MYTHS AND MISCONCEPTIONS ABOUT MONEY FROM THE AFRICAN SKY

TIPS, TRICKS AND SECRETS FOR REACHING FINANCIAL WELLBEING

ZINZI MDEDETYANA

VERVE RAVEN PRESS

The aim of this book is to start a movement to motivate, encourage guide, support consumers to manage(handle) money responsibly like any other challenge out there in their lives. I pray and hope after reading this book, the light will shine upon you; you will take necessary action to change your perspective on your personal finances and be in control and become a leader who continuously moves towards making it a permanent healthy balanced feature of both you & your family's lifestyle.

This book is dedicated to hard-working women and men in South Africa who can identify with and handle limited resources to manage their household, dreams and future endeavors and still hold down their jobs and make a difference in their lives and that of their loved ones and extended families. We salute you for your commitment to keeping hope alive in spite of tough challenges & decisions that you have to endure. Tough times fade away, but, tough people stay resilient at all times and that is, what is inside all of us and we may not recognize it. Robert Frost puts it this way," In three words; I can sum everything I have learned about Life: It goes on". It may feel like you are at the end of your rope; no matter what happens to you, the sun will still rise in the East in the morning and will still set in the West in the evening, so there is hope. Thank you for

inspiring and supporting me, I am indeed eternally
grateful - Zinzi Mdedetyana

I would like to express my heartfelt sincere appreciation to the
following people:

ABBA Father, Jehovah Jireh with your wisdom, when resources
were scarce or non-existent, you provided.

My son Motshwanetsi Ramatlhape who had helped me with the
technological technicalities and meeting demanding and tight
schedules of writing the chapters.

My daughter Masego Ramatlhape my anchor, supporter &
cheerleader behind the scenes
Thank you to both of you for your unfailing & unconditional
love and your continued encouragement. We are a great team
together & nothing will break us.

Joel Ramatlhape - your behind the scene immeasurable&
invaluable support.

My mother Olive Dikeledi Mdedetyana for her prayers,
emotional and financial support, thank you, you are my (s)hero.

My aunt Nontuthuzelo Hlwathi for her emotional support and
the praying warrior.

My adopted daughter Bali Ramatlhape for helping out at short
notice, supporting & encouraged me to go on to write the book,
during the early stages.

My long-time friend Peter Makhambeni for your support, for the lunches, inspirational & encouraging talks.

Sam Tsima long-time friend and confidante, for helping out when things were tough, you didn't know.

Makopano Mothibi for being such a wonderful, supportive, caring person you are.

Maria Sandra Cuasay, my dear friend, pillar of strength, my guide, motivator, dream maker, without which this book would not have been published- you "juiced up" the book to be as lively as it, you are my angel from heaven.

FOREWORD

According to the National Credit Regulator (NCR), the recent statistics show that consumers are experiencing financial distress and finding it difficult to meet their debt commitments monthly, this is the backdrop of where the consumers find themselves.

- There are 25.31 million active credit consumers on credit bureau (register of loans taken up)
- 19.84 million of them have impaired credit records - meaning they are one or more month's behind (in arrears) with one or more or all their accounts and who are experiencing over-indebtedness (overstretched financially and cannot meet their monthly financial obligations), garnishee orders (legal and illegal court orders obtained and issued forcing them to pay back that which is owed to creditors) and other financial burden;
- 45% of consumers have impaired credit records

which means that almost every 4 out of 10
consumers are 3 months or more in arrears (fallen
behind) with their monthly repayments across all
debts (credit cards, overdrafts, personal loans, car,
home including registered micro-lenders).

- 53% of these debtors are aged 31- 45 which means
  that over half of our young members of the
  population are stuck and can't move forward
  because of the debt load(burden) they are facing
  including Black Tax, cannot find jobs(student loans
  burden), cannot start their own businesses(not
  enough resources/financial support) or cannot live
  a decent prosperous life or participate
  meaningfully in the economy.

This is a grave concern as these are our future leaders and
causing many headaches for the government(NCR), National
Treasury & Public Administrations and private companies as
well; over a million or so of the nation is working for the government,
apart from the private sector, so the employers are indirectly
affected, as it affects both private and government service
delivery as many of them cannot perform in their jobs
adequately, fulfilling their mandate of providing goods and
services to society

With over R1.7 trillion that South Africans owed to creditors
in 2019, can you imagine if we were to convert that debt
into savings or investments, how wealthy both the country and
its citizens could become;

- 86% of consumers borrowed money from credit
  providers,
- 75% of consumers owe about 75% of their salaries

to creditors, meaning they wake up every day of
their lives working not only for their employers but
for the people they owe money to - how scary is
that; that is why they do not enjoy their jobs and
their lives;

However, the government through NCR has appointed
Debt Counseling services to assist in rehabilitating highly
distressed consumers by addressing and improving their financial wellbeing and work at reducing these abnormally high
levels of debt load including reckless lending. This topic will be
covered intensely.

I believe by writing this book will go along way to address
some of the deep-seated emotionally charged that is played out,
by historical events including interest rates hikes, increasing
cost of living (inflation), a weak economy, high rates of unemployment, government implementation of certain policies, that
have passed down through generations. There is also guilt,
shame, and humiliation when consumers are distressed and
experiencing disappointment in themselves, letting their loved
ones down; anger, fatigue, anxiety, high-stress levels resulting in
insomnia which further leads to deterioration of health, lower
levels of productivity, absenteeism and sometimes retrench-
ments, as the economy is not growing enough to create sustainable jobs; frequent and increasing conflict with colleagues,
communities, and bosses, lower and falling levels of job satisfaction (paychecks) commitments and loyalty to organization, as so
much time is spent mostly resolving personal financial challenges during working time.

"You cannot move into your tomorrow's with
unresolved yesterday's. You cannot change the single

whisper of yesterday's, but tomorrow is a blank page awaiting your writing on it. Anger will ultimately destroy you. Anger is one letter word away from Danger. Turn your back on the tomb of yesterday and welcome the womb of Today - the womb of possibilities" - David Molapo from his book *Choose to Change*.

Please visit Royalty Ark (https://royaltyark.com). I created Royalty Ark to address these challenges with an understanding that managing personal finances can be intimidating, daunting and scary and downright confusing; so that is why this book is a uniquely tailor-made road map to financial wellbeing and freedom to protect you and your loved one's future.

This book will help you change the way you think about your forgotten downplayed past, and how this has a great influence in affecting your future, therefore by applying lessons, an experience shared in these chapters practical guidelines and exercises that will give you renewed hope to change your life for the better and with that in mind, be careful that "Watch your thoughts for they become your words, Choose your words, for they become actions; Understand your actions, for they become your habits; and your habits they become your character; develop your character, for it becomes your destination" - Anonymous

See this book as a nutrient nourishing medication to your ailing personal finances which is meant to enrich your soul and tells the truth from a place of love and understanding of the situation you find yourself and helps you deal with any financial obstacles you may be facing.

Sometimes the book pulls hard punches, particularly chapters on emotional and some financial sections "stinging like a bee" which may seem harsh and often brutally honest, but it is simple truths and the reason you picked and are reading this book, is that, you have decided to get over the lies that have been told and become an overcomer (to set your heart and mind free).

Segments of these chapters can be read in whole or stand-alone to help focus and tackle a specific area, deliberately, in manageable chunks, especially in areas where it is a battle between your heart and mind and remember we are here to handhold you.

What you put in is what you get out, for you to get more out this book, you have to confront your situation with open-ness, honesty, transparency and with a vision that looks beyond guilt, anger, stress, exhaustion, humiliation, anxiety that sees potential and possibilities and perhaps you have to ask yourself, "What do you have to do to change, to live your dreams on your own terms" - make every second, every minute, every hour, every day, every month, and every year count - baby steps, honey, baby steps, darling, until you summit and conquer that mountain in your life.

———

Extracted from *Choose to Change* by David Molapo, how do we overcome some of these challenges:

- If the stress of being over-indebted, garnishee orders and other financial burdens leave you powerless, angry, anxious and humiliated, then seek professional help rather than relying on wrong advice from colleagues or peers with limited skills, experiences, exposure and that is why we are here to assist.

- Write and share your own story and this will help free your mind and you'll be glad & relieved you did, as you will realize that you're not alone and this will assist you to overcome whatever challenges you're facing and this will allow you to open up to receive assistance and guidance you need.
- You are the director of your own Life(movie); if there's certainly part of your past life that you didn't like, you can either leave it alone or you can use your power and authority to change the lenses(frame) with which you're looking, the part you do not like - change it

Tell yourself, " Today is the first day of the rest of my life"
Ask your loved ones, "What can I do today that would make you enjoy my company"
Ask at work," What can I begin doing today that would allow me to serve you better"
Say this to yourself and mean it," I am beautiful, talented, powerful and I can do anything as there is an inner strength that lies within me" repeat it until it becomes your truth

---

Whenever you feel yourself slipping back into the negative of yesterday; punch a pillow or snap your fingers or shout out loud "No", use a strong visible physical signal as an ON and OFF switch like a WAKE-UP CALL.

Once you have set your goals, start taking active steps to fulfill them. The future is NOW - the steps you take today will determine your destination tomorrow.

We should all be concerned about the future because we will have to spend the rest of our lives there - Charles F. Kettering

ONE

BALANCED WELLBEING

If you always do what you have always done; you will always get what you've always got.

When I engage with my audience, be it addressing a group or holding 1-on-1 coaching sessions or workshops, I always remind them that the path (journey) to financial wellbeing and freedom begins with their thoughts, then heart, then decision, and actions which leads to learnt and practised behaviour. I then ask them to define "insanity" and most of the time I will get empty, blank stares and then an uncomfortable deafening silence that begs for an answer. I almost always give them the answer which is "It is doing the same thing over and over again and expecting different results." Sometimes you wonder why you never grow or move forward and blame it on everything and everyone else except "I", myself, taking responsibility for the outcome.

I go on to explain that for your financial road map to change it has to start with completely new deliberate action (the steps one undertakes) followed by a learnt behaviour (how one acts towards & on those steps) and, finally, thoughts (mind) which will eventually change the way we think and believe towards money. When it comes to money - freedom starts to happen when the head (think) and the heart (emotions) work together in unison. You will have enough money when you take actions to express gratitude and believe that you can be wealthy at any income. So, it is not how much you earn, but how much of it do you keep and grow.

You are more than money, your job, your clothes on your back, your title at work or your 2 or 3 story golf estate house you live in. Your own authentic power and self worth are not judged by what money (profit) can sell and what money can buy; true freedom cannot be bought or sold at any price.

"True financial freedom is that which can never be lost; so true financial freedom is when you have the power over your fears and anxieties and get a realisation, wisdom and appreciation that Life is worth more than the money (net worth) we idolise it to be" - Suze Orman.

It is never too early or too late to begin, no matter how far gone you have been and no matter how your personal bank statement looks or reads today. This journey will help you face the present moment honestly and openly and start to clear the way for you to create the future that you have dreamt of all your life. You must always take a long view of your financial future.

Take the word L-I-F-E. Remove F- (God given freedom &

power from Life) and you are left with a LIE. Instead, learn simple truths and never underestimate or under play the power and authority within you from the Higher Being that says YOU CAN. Until you put belief and action into practice in your own life, you may never know a different, better outcome.

It is also important to understand and accept that your own money has its vibrational energy (up's and down's or ebb's and flow) cycle of life and money.

The Ebb and Flow Cycle of Life and Money

It is important to also understand and accept that your own money has vibrational energy. It's a cycle of life that goes up and down. Sometimes, we plan carefully but life has its own way of unpredictability which is out of our control and unexpected. We are not fully in control of our lives. That is how money also behaves. Sometimes you will have more than enough money in one year and at other times money just vanishes (flows out). These changes can be exciting and at other times fearful. However, they are all part of natural cycle of Life/money.

Sometimes, like in Life, we can plan carefully and with good intentions. However, Life is unpredictable and we are not completely in control of our destiny. The result comes out in a way that seem unexpected. It can be said about money that sometimes you expect more than enough (inherit money from grandparents or parents or get a promotion or win a lottery) and be more fulfilled. At other times money will simply vanish and flow out. You may lose your investments or be retrenched or demoted or fired from your job without warning/reason leaving you with less than you thought. These changes can be exciting and sometimes very fearful, however they are all part of natural cycles of Life or money.

The simple truth is that somehow everything happens to the best of us for a reason. There are no coincidences. During troubled times or when we go through a setback in our lives, we should be able to pull gems (blessings/hidden trea-sures/lessons) and be able to "profit" against all odds even in the toughest experiences and in uncomfortable times. It is through these hard times, that we must learn to be open to new learnings, teachings or lessons and unwrap the gifts that are inner- knowing, the power within us, to enable us to reach out to the outpouring of blessings, prosperity, and riches that you never imagined in your wildest dreams.

The greatest genuine lessons are learnt or can come about during difficult, tough situations when we are in tight corner or deep dark valley that. These simple truths are:

• Money is part of a natural cycle - respect the cycle (process) through learning.
• Gains and losses are built-in and have the capacity to bring us closer to the kind of life we want and dream for a long time.
• Not so good times brings us to the greatest and genuine growth periods. Correcting our past mistakes brings us back to balance.
• Need to be grateful and content and have faith in the cycle of Life and money. It is inner awareness, beliefs, knowledge and authentic power and appreciation that truly create financial freedom.

I WANT you to think back to the worst financial period in your Life that happened to you. How did you feel? Were you anxious, afraid, angry, paralyzed, frustrated, determined to rise up to whatever the world throws at you?

These questions can help to guide your thought processes:

• What happened before the crisis? What caused it?
• What did it feel like during the crisis?
• How did the crisis resolve itself?
• How did it change your Life?
And a few other questions that can trigger your memory:
• Did you ever not get the job or position you really wanted? How did you deal with the blow of not getting it after the sacrifices and hard work you put in?
• Were you ever fired or resigned from your job without knowing where your next income would be coming from?
• Have you ever lost lots of money on get-rich-quick schemes or other investments?
• Have you ever had a relationship break up and also be very worried about money?
• Have you ever had a friendship (relationship) end over money?
• When and why in your Life were you the most fearful about money?

Write down your story. It may help you to deal or handle openly both your excitement and your fears. You will feel relieved and empowered and once you do that, you can destroy your "old story."

Start on a new clean slate. Forgive yourself for the past mistakes you have made. Reclaim your inner power and start a new journey to financial wellbeing and freedom!

Well Done.
We've got
your back!

TWO

MEASURE OF SELF WORTH

It is not so much how busy you are, but why you are busy that counts. The bee is praised; the mosquito is swatted. - Mary O'Connor

Let me ask you a question. What does true financial freedom or true wealth mean to you? What do you value most in your Life? Is it money or Life? Pause and think about it before you answer it for yourself.

In the meantime, here is my answer for you. Financial freedom is not within our pay slips, our fancy and fast Sports Utility Vehicle (SUV), our comfortable homes in an exclusive private golf estate, our branded clothes, our available balance at our bank, our investments or our spending spree at shopping malls. I will say that we cannot measure our self worth by how much money, savings and investments you have accumulated over the years. Our assets can make life easier but they can be wiped out overnight. I do not have to remind you of Enron in America and recently here in South Africa - African Bank in 2014, Steinhoff in 2017 and a few others around the world. Pension funds and shareholder interests with billions of savings came crashing down like a house of cards blown apart by the wind. If we define self worthiness in that fashion, then we are lying to ourselves.

What is true financial freedom? It is who we are, the power we possess within, the inner knowing, the confidence, the assurance and above all the core centre of our being. It is the richness and worthiness that come from within when a state of true contentment, true happiness and true gratefulness has been reached. The true core of who you are will attract true wealth and eventually financial freedom. That my friend is PRICELESS.

Do this exercise at home. Pretend you're holding a garage sale and put a price tag on each item in your "store." This is the price that you initially paid for it. Include your TV set/screen, couches, dining table & chairs, carpets, fridge, washing machine, dish washer, clothes, shoes, bags, your car and any other things of value. Put a second tag with the price you believe it is worth today. This is the price you would sell it for.

I must admit this exercise also helps to reveal how much "stuff" we accumulate over the years. Sometimes these are things we never use again. Yet, we say we need it and we'll use it or wear it one day and that day never comes. It rots or collects dust or breaks off.

Separate those ordinary items from those that really create memories in your heart(sentimental value as we call it). Affix a price tag, for example, wedding rings, washing machine, a family painting, clothes or shoe bags. Now, the question is, what price tag will those heartfelt items have?

What we really would like to know is, what price tag would you put on your Life? Is your Life defined by the accumulation of all these things you have set aside as sentimental? Is this what self worth is all about to you? ~ Suze Orman

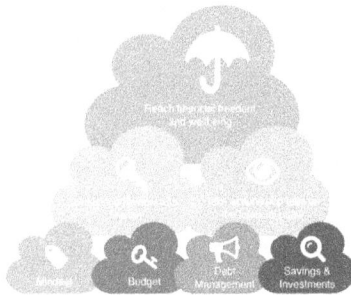

I hope and trust that this chapter has touched you to the core making you think and question more about the real reason of what true self worth truly is. In our busy lives, we learn that money has an awesome power. It is capable of doing amazing, wonderful things for ourselves and others. It can also create fearful moments that paralyze us into indecision.

Money can also bring joy and abundance from one generation to the next. It can be given to causes great and small to help others. This can only happen with awareness, wisdom and practice. The responsible and wise sowing and nurturing of money will always yield the most satisfying harvest. But a harvest never planted, shall never grow.

Use your time now to learn how to plant your financial field. Learn what steps to take to assure growth and health over time. Learn to adapt for good times and bad.

Keep the hope alive. Keep reading.

Well Done. Keep On Moving!

THREE

SEEING YOUR PAST STRONGHOLDS

Being open and honest with yourself is the first step to receive and accept your truth. You can start today. It is a choice. With time your new narrative (rewriting your script) will change. It will not be overnight, but in time it will change. - Zinzi Mdedetyana

I want to share my personal financial journey. I remember the first encounter I had with money. My first lasting impression of money was when I was eight or nine years old. I am not proud of what I did. I used to sneak into my father's bedroom (please forgive me) and took coins, especially 20c or 50c, from my late father's trouser pockets. I did this to buy myself sweets and treats because I never have spare cash. I could also show off to my friends at school. They would see that I have lots of money to splash around. In hindsight, I admit that it was never a good idea. Please, father, forgive me for I have sinned.

Another bad memory was when I was 14 or 15 years old.

There was a school field trip to Mpumalanga (one of our 9 provinces in South Africa). I really wanted to go but my father declined my request. I was so sad, humiliated and embarrassed. I really wanted to be with my friends and my boyfriend at the time. My boyfriend even offered to pay for my trip but my father again said, "No." He never told me why. From that day on I vowed to work hard to have my own money and riches and not to depend on anyone.

Believe you me, during school vacations, I would work. My first job was at a retail clothing stores called Sales House (now part of Edgars Group) as a floor consultant and sometimes as a cashier at the tills. I would make so many mistakes such as shortages that I would be removed from tills and returned to serving customers on the floor. I enjoyed that much more than handling cash.

With the money I earned, I would spoil myself like going to movies alone. Some of the money I would save. I remember that I thought and said to myself that I want to be so rich that I would not want to be a beggar for the rest of my life. At the time, I thought and convinced myself that life was all about money.

I asked my mother to help me open up a savings account at First National Bank (FNB). I planned to save my money and become wealthy. That was all that mattered in my mind back then. It drove me and laid a foundation of paralyzed insecurities about money in the future.

When I was at college studying towards my first Auditing Diploma qualification in my final year, I worked on weekends at Claremont Woolworths retail store in Cape Town as a temp. It was not great income but enough to meet my needs as a student. I would buy some food and treats and bring it back to the dormitory to show off that I have money to feed myself. Those who came to visit me came to realize that they never went hungry visiting my room. I always had money. It made me feel liberated and secure.

But it was wrong. I was doing it from a place of fear that paralyzed me instead of from love and appreciation. Fear had such a strong hold on me that I always worked hard. I was also lucky to get well paying jobs and consistently achieved more than my peers. I would have a job and other sideline businesses. I did not realize that this stronghold of fear was paralyzing me. I was stuck frozen into one pattern of thinking and behaving.

I did not dream about other possibilities. I did not seek opportunities to become a better person. My sense of security was tied to having a job and money. I did not realize that my vision of myself was limited by where I was in life professionally and financially.

There is my story. Now tell me your story, dreams and goals.

Reviewing your Past Strongholds

"By visiting your past, you are able to unearth and uncover mistakes made and be able to move forward with confidence".

By visiting your past strongholds it is nothing to be embarrassed or ashamed of, instead see it as an opportunity to understand your past limited beliefs (you did not know any better). You need to **forgive yourself** for all the sums of the decisions you have undertaken with the limited view mirror/lenses with which you were viewing your life, your decisions, your limited knowledge. Now, you know better you are in the light and you cannot go back and claim that you did not know. By visiting our past we lift ourselves of deep seated wounds and regret.

What Are Your Goals

These can be about financial freedom, financial power, healthy decisions, personal relationships and other things you want in your own life.

• I want to pay off my debts and get out for good.

• I want to make sure that there will be enough money for my children's education.

• I want to retire in 10 years and never to work for a Boss ever again.

• Being able to afford the lifestyle I want without having to work hard to achieve it.

• I want to be confident that my family will be provided for, if something happens to me.

• I want to travel the world over.

• I want to know that my parents and siblings can afford to have medical aid/insurance as they get older or unemployed.

• I desire the freedom to use my TIME to do what I want when and where I want to do it, with whom I want to do it.

Remember, you did not come to this world to breath air, pay bills and die. You came to this world to make a difference by leaving an indelible mark or a proud legacy. You may do this whilst you enjoy, love, give, be, do and have all of life's delicious, exhilarating moments.

FEAR

• How will I pay for my children's higher and further education expenses?

• I am afraid I will lose everything I have and my friends & relatives will find out how much money I have, they would laugh(make fun of me) and it would be embarrassing/humiliation for me and my children, so I have to cover up(sugarcoat) my life and show off that I can afford whilst I cannot even buy essential necessities for my family. What will I do?

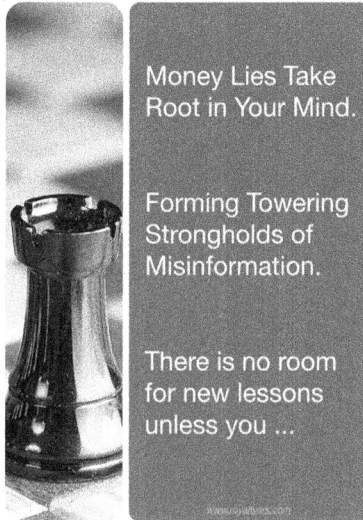

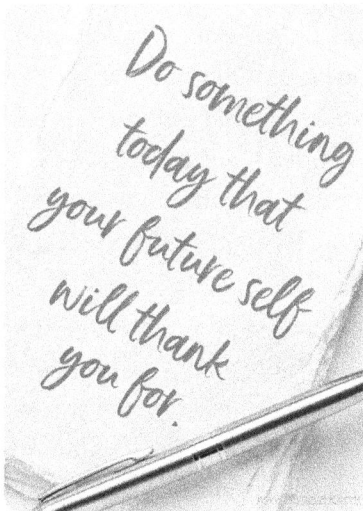

Money Lies Take Root in Your Mind.

Forming Towering Strongholds of Misinformation.

There is no room for new lessons unless you ...

Do something today that your future self will thank you for.

POSITIVE TRUTHS

• I am in control of all my Life's current and future affairs.

• I have more money than I will ever need; I am receiving truckloads of money everyday, thank you, thank you, Universe I receive; money loves me and I love money (remember money has vibrational energy) and this is the power of words.

• I am putting at least R500,00 a month into my savings account.

Ask these questions to yourself:

• Is it time or fear that stops (hinder) me from dealing with your financial situation honestly or openly?

• What does it really costs me to live each month(fixed life-style expenses)? Sometimes we find that these expenses are always omitted from the budget exercise(spending pattern plan), so that it seems to "look good" and yet we are not seeing the real clear picture.

Regular expenses: should also include weekly expenses such as movies, smoking, wine & spirits, eating out (burg-ers/chips/chicken finger-lickin good/pizza), airtime (data bundles) over time i.e. weekly, monthly and yearly.

Variable expenses: should also include magazine, internet, subscriptions, cosmetics (nails & hairdo), car service & repairs not covered by vehicle insurance, braai, visitors from church or hang around common friends every week, month, year over time.

Special occasions expenses: should include festivals, awards ceremonies, Christmas vacations and holidays, baby showers attended, presents, flowers wine bottles bought, anniversaries, weddings, birthdays, dinner dates including Valentine's day, house warming parties, week- end- get- away, and how much it costs.

Obtain your bank statement and salary advice over six months up to one year. Ask yourself how much of it have you spent, saved and paid over to third parties. I always say, there is nothing that does not lie like your bank statement as it reveals your spending habits. We can track how and where your money went.

Decide how much you plan to spend in each category (preference allocation choice). Doing this gives you control over spending instead of limiting what you can spend. The Personal Spending Planner™ reflects your dreams and work towards it.

Remember, it is "a journey to a destination that you would have defined for yourself; not around the harbour - going around and around in circles."

FOUR

EMOTIONAL RELATIONSHIP TO MONEY

It is not the load that breaks you down. It is the way
you carry it. - Lena Horne

What kind of relationship do you have with money? Is it positive or negative? If it is positive then great for you because you're well on your way to financial wellbeing and freedom. Perhaps, you can stop and not read this chapter any further or perhaps you can pass it on to someone who may benefit from it.

For those of us who were not so fortunate to have a prosperous start in life, then this chapter is dedicated to you. Let us take a trip down memory lane and discover for ourselves when, how and why did it all start and how can you change this narrative that does not define who you are and what you become.

Emotional Relationship to Money

(Expectation, Desires vs Reality)

"An unsavory relationship with money entered into with naivety
results in unintended consequences"

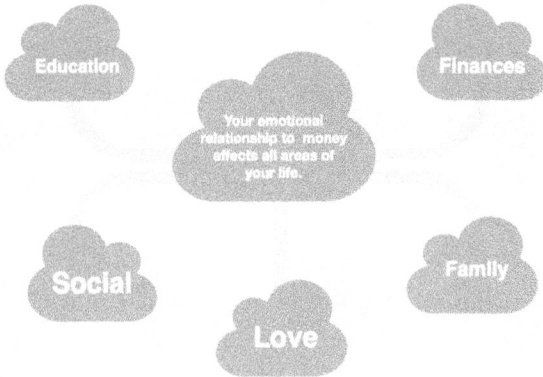

Education

Finances

Your emotional
relationship to money
affects all areas of
your life.

Social

Family

Love

Unfortunately, when we were young, money was not a subject easily, openly and comfortably discussed at our dinner table in our household. This was especially true of the descendants of African origin. Perhaps, it may be true for other nationalities. Money was a fuzzy, do-not-touch something that was fascinating. Yet like an elusive lover better hidden and unremarked, money was kind of a phenomenon.

I guess it was also that narrative that because all we had was love that glued us together, money was referred to "imali iyimpande yesono" translated loosely as "money is the root to all evil", especially in the Christian family background that we were all brought up with and grew accustomed to. Sometimes when we asked for money, parents would respond this way, "Do you think money grows on trees?" We would stop asking fearing our parents' response and attitude. We were indirectly influenced to fear the the subject of money and taught to leave it alone. The fear and discomfort of discussing money began. We grew up thinking that it does not need the attention it deserves. Money conflicts were to be avoided at all cost to keep the peace. But, deep down in our gut, there was always this lurking curiosity about it.

Reality reared it ugly ears when we started working as young professionals. Personal financial challenges began to come to the fore. We misunderstood/mismanaged/misappropriated the very resource that we were taught (molded) to avoid. It is no wonder we are battling to keep and earn more. When we have more of it we boast bling, bling about it. The way we spend money comes from lessons of yesterday and today. We keep or save too little because, unfortunately and truth be told, no one sat us down and gave us a personal Financial Management Experience 101 (Stewardship). We could have learned and understood the values and principles to manage this most "feared demonic monster." It would have made our lives easier allowing us to achieve our life's goals, desires and dreams. Without this knowledge, we are tossed from one side to another. We feel confused, suffocated and stressed with our own emotions (guilty feelings of inadequacy) because we cannot handle this resource properly.

Lacking knowledge, we mimicked and rarely asked questions. Misbehaviour was prevalent in our communities when money was available. People would buy expensive booze, clothes, shoes and furniture to numb the pain and disappointment. Only for these things to be later repossessed. They would show disrespect towards spouses & children by mistreating them and withholding financial assistance. What little was left would be collected as stokvel (pulling community). But this too would be depleted by years end Christmas expenses.

A few enlightened individuals would exercise what I call "consumption saving." They would save just enough funds to cover school fees and holiday expenses. This is a good strategy but not ideal. If they only understood how powerful and wise they could become had they invested in stokvel consistently, they would be ahead in their lives.

Unfortunately, our African folks were not educated and shown how they could pull & grow their monies (investment) beyond that, few "accidentally read" financial books/magazines which was neither real, nor resonated nor practical for our folk (if they were lucky to come across and read them and take them earnestly to try to put into practice) as it was written for a certain class of the society and, bear in mind, our folks were excluded in participating in the economy. In all honesty, our African folk were not allowed to become economically free (save, invest, start their own businesses) by our previous Apartheid government, those who broke the laws (rules) paid a handsome hefty price on their lives by taking risks. I do not downplay and blame them at all, they did what they knew and experienced then, but facing our demons of the past we must not lose the lesson though; however we need to move beyond our past (as it does not define us) and create a future for our beloved one's that is prosperous and free and not continue with past bad beaten learnings that leads us to nowhere slowly.

Yet to our surprise our fears are confirmed, desires, dreams come crushing down as a self fulfilling prophesy, as we believe there is not enough go around, so we kill each other for it, as we believe that it (fortune) only favours the brave, so we become jealous (envious) and hate those who seem to "have more than enough" and live the lifestyle that we can only dream of. We go on believing and telling ourselves same old story, that it is "our lot". We will never be prosperous, we will never move forward and have enough and it seems that it will stay that way for generations to come. We begin to hate ourselves. We become hurt, guilty, disappointed, stressed, and depressed (all those feelings come together all at once). This negativity begin to affect our health, our lives and the whole outlook on life - we lose hope. I call it the power of words and thought patterns. We live to become what our words, thoughts and deeds command us, in the way we conduct ourselves and our lives (speak, behave/posture, walk and how we see and live life).

If you haven't the ability to impose your own terms on life, you must accept the terms it offers you. ~ T.S. Eliot.

If we want to see a different outcome, as it is not the past that defines us, it is where we are going that will make the shift; so we have to change our "old narrative/story" that it is not supposed to convict us, money is a means to an end and not an end in itself and it is an exchange for something that we desire, love, dream of, as an end goal and it should not occupy so much "airtime" in our minds and daily speech to an extent of obsessions (as if we cannot live without it) in fact we can. We all have access to this resources equally and fairly, the myth is that we believe it is for the privileged few. We should not entertain thoughts of lack (not enough) instead we should be thinking pure positive thoughts towards money, as if it were more than enough, in abundance, Right now and it is continuously flowing easily and effortlessly.

All we need to do is to cultivate in ourselves values, principles, guidelines and understanding of universal laws that govern not only money, but everything else that we want to have, be or do in our lives; that would assist us to attract money and more of it, good long pleasurable, exhilarating, blessed life that we have been given not for some, but, for ALL OF US, and not repel it, as it is there for the taking.

• What are your values & principles towards money?

• Do you understand, value and respect it? Did you know that it has a vibrational energy?

• Are you transparent in how you spend it (spending patterns)?

• Do you account for your actions and inaction when spending or not spending it (hoarding it)?

• Do you even have a plan on how to save, spend and increase your income potential (hobbies)?

• Do you appreciate what it can do for you or do you grumble and complain all the time when it is not around/there?

• Do you just spend it ALL and then hope and pray that somehow miraculously it will solve itself and somehow last forever?

If you answered "YES" to most of the questions then, congratulations you are aware of how to value and respect money. If your responses was mostly "NO", then you need to develop new positive truths about money by appreciating and being grateful for the things that money can buy for your daily needs (start by instilling, installing new belief system in your mind) and then see what happens. It is a whole new world out there.

For me, Personal Financial Wellness, has everything to do

with financial wellbeing, balance & freedom to be, to live, to do and to have whatever my heart desires "without breaking the bank", as the Americans would say. I read a disturbing statistic (trend) from the National Credit Regulator (NCR) with over 23,9 million active consumers (what was worrying for me was the 53% of these consumers aged 31-45, very young women and men of our society) who are over-indebted (cannot fulfill their monthly obligations & live freely) and they apply poor money management principles and it galvanized (gave me courage) to put this book together to start a movement, change the narrative (rewrite the history), influence people to handle money efficiently and effectively and with proper tender loving care and guidance, so that we can get the outcome that we wish for.

VISIT your Financial Wellbeing home at www.royaltyark.com and meet your Mentor/Coach. Read on and let us engage. I have put chapters together that cover details on how you can change your outlook and become empowered on your journey to personal finances. Please read on.

I want to end this chapter with these words. We all have an incredible capacity for handling any challenges that life throws at us and the capability (potential) to become powerful, far much greater than what we can see for and in ourselves, so money should not be the only determining factor in your life, because you are more than your money, your job, your unemployment, your clothes, your important title, your fancy & fast car, your double/triple story house in a safe golf estate - just see it as a means to end, not an end in itself. We have a Higher Being or the Universe that loves, cares for us deeply and always gazes upon us and who, however, you see or understand of Him; He provided for you before you were born, He still provides even in your sleep and will provide until you are old (with your gray hairs), so money should not be an obsession that you can neither have enough sleep, nor peace and nor rest over it. Live your Life joyfully, peacefully, deliberately and enjoy your own journey on your own terms.

FIVE

NEEDS VS WANTS

Bare necessities of life, the simple bare necessities, forget about your worries and stress. I mean bare necessities, your Mother's nature's recipes that brings the bare necessities of Life" - Phil Harris & Bruce Reitherman

---

Needs refers to basic necessities for our own survival and existence such as the air that we breathe, food, shelter (housing), simple clothes (not bling, bling), education and proper basic cleanliness & hygiene. Remember, cleanliness is next to godliness. Once all the basic needs are met, we are fulfilled no matter what our situation or whatever is going on in our lives.

On the other hand, Wants are usually unplanned and driven by the selfish impulses of greed and envy. We find ourselves competing with and comparing ourselves with other people and their possessions. We ignore our own current circumstances and capabilities. In essence, we are living our dreams through others. Wants have to do with "future desires" which cannot be met just NOW. But they can be achieved with proper planning and working towards that goal over time. It is the accumulation of "stuff" that we really do not need and can live without.

The main reason (there could many reasons) why we confuse the two concepts is that we lack self control, proper planning, patience, flawed decision-making process & review. We live in an instant microwaveable life where everything MUST happen NOW on our timetable - instant gratification. If it does not happen NOW, we lose our cool and our minds. We force it to happen by ALL MEANS POSSIBLE. We do not care who gets hurt along the way while we get whatever we want at all cost. Usually those things or "stuff" cause so much distress, misery and pain. In the end, we are neither happy nor enjoy our lives. We wish we never had it.

Self Control is a choice, not a feeling. Let us use an example to illustrate this. You know that when we eat too much of our favourite food or drink of any kind it leads to discomfort (tummy ache or headaches or sleeplessness or restlessness) because we have indulged or we have taken in excess of what we our bodies could handle. But we continue to binge because we want to impress, defy or ignore the consequences. Later, in amazement, we wonder what had really happened. We blame everyone else around. We do not point at Self, and ask the right questions - what got me here, or how did I get here, or why am I here?

We avoid the answer like plague, because we "avoid" getting the appropriate answer that will help solve the problem. We continue down the same spiral path of defiance and ignorance as if nothing wrong has happened. With little thought, indulgence resumes and the cycle continues until we reach a point of no return resulting in disappointment, the blame game, anger, stress, depression and even suicidal thoughts. We play the help-less victim mentality game and do not take any early action and wishing, hoping & praying that the problem will go away. Unfortunately it never does until we face it squarely in its face and deal with it.

This has to do with our beliefs, behaviour and attitude towards the money that we work so hard for yet can hardly keep or manage it. Remember money has a vibrational energy. You grumble and complain about the lack of it and so it disappears from your hands. We need to develop a different mode of thinking and behaving towards money.

Needs vs Wants(Where is the Confusion?)

Self-control is the new currency of CHOICE!

How we treat money has to do with thinking differently, CHOICES not FEELING towards it. Act on it and not REACT to it. When we deal with choices we look into the reality of the situation at hand, not what we would like to imagine or wish it to be.

Open Up The Truth Lid

Self-control is a choice and not a feeling. Transparent & Be money wise.

IF WE WANT to effect a different outcome, we must begin to be aware and study our CHOICES and not our emotions. Here we talk about the reality of the situation at hand and not what we would like to see, to be or to do. Let me give you an example to clarify the point. If I earn R5000,00 per month, I cannot compete or compare myself with an educated friend who earns R50,000.00 per month. Our age, education, position, needs, wants and lifestyle (achievements) are not the same and they NEVER will be the same. I advise STOPPING for a moment and applying your mind properly. Realize that you should run your own RACE. Stick to your own path and destination. Frankly, I do not know how my educated friend earned that R50 000,00 and what activities he conducted to earn that kind of money. He will not tell me even if I beg him for information. He only brags about it.

I am not saying that you will never achieve the status or income of my educated friend. With vigour, focus, armed with a good plan and clear SMART goals & vision for your life, I believe You CAN. You see, if you look at the word LIFE and you remove the letter "F", what are you left with "LIE" and that is exactly what you experience, a lie to yourself, your family and loved one's because you are running someone else's race, and not yours and that brings & invites all sorts of unintended consequences, so stick with your path and run. In time you will reach your goals. As they say, "Rome was never built in one day".

Just like the fastest man, Hussein Bolt, when he runs his race, he never looks to his left, his right or behind. Like his name, he bolts like a horse, focused FORWARD. Truth be told, he is not competing or comparing himself with his fellow athletes. He is competing with his personal best time.

So, if we can start to use the teaching in that example, we will see the changes in our Lives. There is always help (coach, mentor, guide) out there - ready and willing to assist. The challenge is PRIDE which has taken over and holds us back like a slow poison. It is killing and destroying our society, especially the fibre of our families, and prevents us from moving forward to reach our financial and life goals.

The worst and sometimes uncomfortable and bitter pill to swallow is to face the "demon" head on with the intention to be truthful and open. We desire to find a permanent lasting solution where we must live within our means in the NOW so it becomes a way of Life. If we do so, we will be living the Life that is content we were meant to live peacefully, joyfully, and enjoying the journey to a selected final destination.

SIX

LIFE'S STAGES - UNDERSTANDING THE LIFE CYCLE

We all go through ages, stages and changes in our lives and Life is constantly changing and throwing curve balls at us and at times unpredictable; so we need to be prepared at all times. We need to identify important Life events that might happen over the course of our Lives and depending on the Life stages we find ourselves in; we need to plan for it, as to avoid disappointments (consequences of poor financial planning, guilt and anger) for the rest of our Lives.

During the course of Life, we come across unforeseen events that will affect your life, your budget and financial planning. These events will not only affect your finances, but could also have an impact your health which ends up costing so much more, so what do you do?

Your financial goals will change as you go through different and important landmarks and milestones of your life. However, no matter who you are and where you are in Life, it is up to you to take charge and manage your own finances. It will not happen by default or accident, you need to work at it. You must remain in control and be aware of your financial milestones (such life events and be able to tackle unforeseen events) at all times.

We are here to help, guide and chart out tips which may be different from one person to another and from one stage (age) to another. It may not fit your Life perfectly as everyone is different. At least think of it as a financial checklist that is quick reminder/reference guide of what needs to be considered as we go through these life stages.

You need to have clear financial goals, by taking a SMART APPROACH. Firstly, let us explain what short, medium and long term goals mean.

• Short term goals refers to goals (things, dreams, desires, wants) that you want to achieve within the shortest period of time, e.g. 12-24 months. This could mean enrolling for a short course in Personal development or paying off the least amount of debt.

• Medium term goals refers to goals that you would like to achieve within 3-5 years such as returning to school for a 3 years degree or masters qualification or buying a car.

• Long term goals refers to goals (dreams, desires, wants,

things) that you would have liked to have had within 5-30 years such as buying a house, investing in stocks or tax savings or building a successful business in this market and in this industry.

To have the highest chance of success, all these goals must be SMART.

S - Specific. Your goals must be clear and detailed as much as possible in your mind; e.g. I want to be debt free by the end of 2024 and take my first overseas trip to Brazil in 2025 and pay for it CASH.

M - Measurable. You need to always check how and what you are doing in line with achieving your goal, e.g. I will start paying an extra R500.00 towards my short term debt to kill both the interest and balance (capital).

A - Achievable. You need to do and also consider whether you can do it to achieve your goal; e.g I must cut unnecessary spending and start paying more towards my debt

R - Realistic. Your goal must be something that you truly believe you can do it supported by a strong will power to do it to achieve, e.g. I cannot afford to take on more debt, as I am heading towards being debt free. For the next 2 years I should clear all my short term debt and be able to board a flight to Brazil in 2025 paid for by CASH!

T - Time bound/Time-related. You need to set time lines or expiration dates for your goals; e.g. I want to be financially independent by the end of 2024. Firstly, establish what your monthly income can pay. Please read this in conjunction with The Road map to financial well being Chapter 13 as it includes an overview of tracking where your money goes (income and expenses and debt). You need to consider saving for retirement (pension, provident fund), disability, estate planning, medical, funeral and life policies.

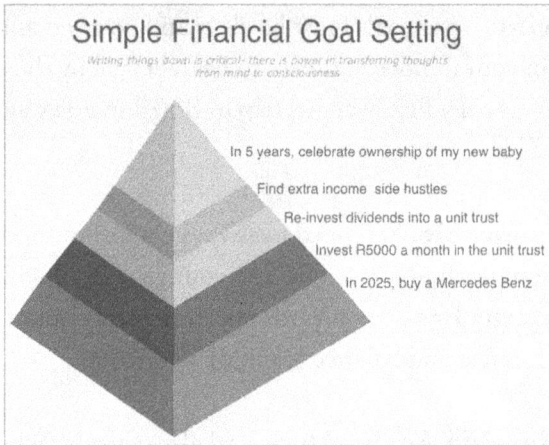

Simple Financial Goal Setting

Writing things down is critical- there is power in transforming thoughts from mind to consciousness

In 5 years, celebrate ownership of my new baby

Find extra income side hustles

Re-invest dividends into a unit trust

Invest R5000 a month in the unit trust

In 2025, buy a Mercedes Benz

With regards to retirement, if your company provides for pension plans and provident funds, make sure you take them up. Also consider putting a little extra cash into retirement annuities (RA) which are accessible from age 55 to provide for retirement. Our government cannot continue paying for pensions to people who worked previously. The government now encourages employees to buy retirement annuities instead of joining the SASSA (South African Social Security Services) grant queue (Government pension).

One should see retirement as investing in your future and getting in early to start saving for retirement which is the best gift you can ever give to yourself and your loved one's, to ensure you have enough money to live comfortably and the way we live our retirement days should continue as, how we lived our productive lives. Retirement planning involves much more than finances. You have to decide when to retire; where will you live; and what will you be doing. These decisions depends on the income you can expect to earn before or during your retirement years. Planning for retirement is a long term process and requires time, effort and careful considerations to reach your decision.

You'll will need to engage the help of a Financial Planner who has your best interest at heart and who looks at your retirement savings as part of financial planning.The reason pension or provident funds exist is to provide employees and their dependents (beneficiaries) a financial future with a guaranteed income upon retirement or death. Although, there are other vehicle options available, a retirement fund is probably the best option investment vehicle for many employed investors to save towards their unproductive years where there's no more income coming in. It all depends on the strategy and cost structure of the investment vehicle you take. Please take the necessary precautionary measures when handling this subject. You will be grateful you took the time to seriously consider your options.

The main difference between pensions and provident funds is that:

Pension Fund: The pension will be paid out until you die and offers individuals better tax benefits to the employee.

Provident Fund: It is usually more flexible than pension fund in that part of the lump sum can be used to buy a private pension such as a Retirement Annuity through a private pension company. Again the difference is also how you receive your fund at retirement.

When the member retires, when they belong to a pension fund, the member can take up to a third of the total benefit in a cash lump sum, and the other 2/3 is paid out in monthly installments in the form of a pension over the rest of the member's life. This monthly income will be taxed at your average rate of taxation in retirement. If no cash lump sum is taken, then the full benefit will be paid monthly resulting in a higher monthly pension.

If you are a member of a provident fund, then the member can get the full benefit paid in a cash lump sum. A portion of this would be tax free, but the rest of the lump sum will be taxed.

If you resign from your employer, please do not cash out your fund (you are stealing from your future), you can transfer your pension or provident fund to a fund of your new employer or into a Retirement Annuity or to a Preservation Fund and the good news is that, you will not be taxed on the transfer of the fund (savings) to any of these investment vehicles and you are allowed one withdrawal before transfer or retirement.

How do Retirement Annuities (RA's) work: Annuities are an insurance product (often used as an investment option) any individual will need in any age and any stage of their Life stages and Life events (mitigating risks that affect your financial planning) that must be planned for; so they provide a source of income during retirement. Unlike life insurance, an annuity makes payment while the person is still alive. Other people who can benefit by using an annuity are for self employed or employees whose earnings towards retirement or employees whose organizations do not provide pension or provident fund.

The benefit of Retirement Annuity is that it can also be used, as mentioned before, to accommodate transfers of lump pension or provident sum fund (savings) when leaving (moving) in between jobs.The government is now encouraging South African citizens to buy RA's over and beyond their normal pensions, to compliment their income, after retirement, to lesson the burden of paying grants, government pensions and allow the citizens to take care of themselves and stop relying on government.

RA's are tax- friendly investment vehicles, please note that an individual cannot withdraw funds from RA before the age of 55; however, if the entire benefit amount is less than R7000,00; the funds can be withdrawn.

By now, you should know that savings and investment in retirement should ideally begin immediately when you start your first job and should continue until your later life just before retirement. You also know that life also throws curve balls and that important life events happen over the course of your life that may change (happen) unexpectedly; therefore your investment strategy will also change according to the life stages experienced. It is important to consider factors that may affect your investment strategy, such as how much investment (retirement) is invested, as it will affect the end result; as to whether you'll have a safe or tumultuous landing(retirement) that my friend is the choice you make.

Age

• *20's and 30's: Young and promising:* As a young and upcoming, you have a unique opportunity, as you maybe still single, moved out of the parent's house(still living with them) and just started your first job; you can consider to become more aggressive with your investment strategy; as you have a unique position and many years to weather the storms(market up's and down's).

• *40's and 50's:* Climbing the career ladder and getting solid career-married and parenthood - As you change jobs; getting hungry for the next level of your career such as getting married have kids; always negotiating a better salary thus earning more each time and over your lifetime; it presents an opportunity to live pretty well and also save and invest extra cash(channel some money into savings and investment instead of blowing it all on living now). Consider using growth and income investment approach to help balance retirement planning and other larger financial commitments such as children's education, home and investing in estate planning. The good news is that you still have enough time to grow your nest egg.

• *60's and 70's:* Take it easy - You have made it to the end of your working life (approaching retirement) and can now enjoy with little work stress and more time with grandchildren and other family members. As you no longer receive regular income and you're living (relying) on your savings and investment, so you need to be on top of your budget (must be read in conjunction with Chapter 8 Roadmap to Financial Wellbeing). Review your investments regularly and consider your risk tolerance (reduce risk in your investment portfolio as there will be little time to recover any losses NOW). If you take a BIG loss now on the money you have saved; it would be a disaster and might lead to living with consequences of poor financial planning for the rest of your life.

• *70's and beyond:* Survivor - If you or your loved one (partner/spouse and children) passed away, it is important that the surviving family members are well prepared for the life's journey without them; so no need to be anxious (worry) just speak/approach your financial advisor to make sure that all is still well and according to plan, you had as a couple, and perhaps some changes must be done according to the wishes of the surviving spouse, and, you may still have some insurance payout or pension fund payout or retirement annuity payout, so spend it wisely; so you need to make sure that your assets keep working for you through your retirement and that your investment portfolio is more conservative (reduce or eliminate risks altogether than ever before)

Gender

We have observed and we are seeing it, that women outlive men and in most times, they are the breadwinners of homes and therefore they must save and invest more for longer.

Retirement Date

The regulated retirement age in South Africa is 65, however most people retire two or 3 years earlier, or younger, so if you decide to retire earlier you will have to consider that you may need more money to retire on. Perhaps, this is the best time to start considering enlisting your God given talents (gifts), put them to best use, if you retire early.

Dependents

Consider the number of dependents and their life stages that you have, before and in retirement years, as it will affect the amount of contributions and capital you will need to save before retirement and that you will need in retirement.

Savings

The more you have in savings besides your retirement, the less you will need or more conservatively within your retirement fund choices and decisions; however engage (speak) to a Financial Planner and/or do your homework before saving and investing, so that you can live a comfortable retirement years and life with minimal stress.

Steps to Consider

WHEN YOU INVEST your money you need to consider between many and different options. Some yield faster growth but are more and high risk; others offer slow growth, yet conservative growth; so you can decide where your hard earned money goes and how much risk you are willing to take on (risk/appetite). Do your homework before investing but you should not be overwhelmed or scared. You are already on your way to winning the race and building your real wealth.

Understand what is happening in the economy. Educate yourself read business papers, watch the news, the more clued up you are about what is happening both in the local and global economy, the better and more empowered you are to make smart decisions about your money, that would allow you to avoid disappointments. A great idea is for you to approach or engage a good and reliable Financial Planner (advisor) to take care of your investments. Armed with relevant and accurate information (facts), you could never go wrong. Just as an example, if the economy is not doing well, it is advisable to invest in bonds as they tend to to do well in downturn; when the economy is booming then find yourself good stocks (shares) and commodities (such as gold, precious metals, platinum) as good investments.

Stay calm in stormy economic seas. As we all know local and global economies do not remain the same, they change all the time. A bad day in South Africa (SA) may mean a good day in the United States of America (USA) or vice versa and so it means that you should not panic where your investments are invested; there will always be Highs and Lows (slumps as brokers call it) you ride the rough seas (waves). Stay calm and informed. Talk to your Financial Advisor if you believe that you should adjust your investment portfolio.

Discipline is the name of the game. To win this investment game, you need to commit a certain amount monthly and consistently. The earlier you begin the investment process, the better and the larger your investment fund will be in the future. Setting a target ensures that you are deliberate and will be forced to invest and stay on track towards your future investment.

SEVEN

CONSIDER LIFE EVENTS

Unforeseen events and risks - understand how it all affect you and your financial planning, so you cannot predict what your life has to offer and how it will eventually pan out, but you need to plan for it, as your finances could have an impact on them, otherwise life will happen to you. - Old Mutual

---

I would like to address different kinds of short and long term insurance products that are available to you. You may take them up as your circumstances dictate or requires of it. However, it would be foolish NOT to have insurance to take care of any eventualities and emergencies that you may experience as you go through the various stages of your life.

- Your health, e.g. old age, chronic diseases
- Loss of your house
- You might have to take out a loan at high interest rate from micro lender.
- You may have an additional expenses, e.g. further education for your children.
- Your death might leave your family financially devastated.
- Medical problems/disability can leave you out of pocket/job

Insurance is there to protect you from unforeseen life events as well as from some events that we know will happen (such as death) but do not know when it will strike; so the insurance company agrees to take the risk and insure you for a certain specific amount, time period, with certain conditions.

The difference between short term and long term insurance is that long term insurance focuses on covering life over the longest period of time. Short term insurance covers anything you own over a short period of time, for instance, 12 - 72 months, with certain conditions.

Funeral Policy

It is aimed at protecting you from unforeseen or unexpected expensive funerals to bury a loved one. It usually pays out on the death of the insured person including beneficiaries who may receive a lump sum amount which is usually established upfront(upon signing the documents/contractual agreement)

Disability Insurance

Sometimes also called income protection; this type of insurance covers you if you become disabled during your active working life, where your disability causes you to stop working, it then protects the income you would have earned, had you been active (able to work). It pays out to the insured person becoming disabled.

Life Insurance

It is a contract between the insurer (usually the insurance companies) and the insured (usually you and me) where you promise to pay regular premiums or as a lump sum for the policy; where the insurer promises to pay out a nominated beneficiary (usually children, spouses, parents) a sum of money upon the death of the insured person(you). Because these kinds of contracts involve large sums of money; please read the fine print(T's &C's), as there will be cases where the insurer may not pay out, e.g. in a case where the insured committed suicide, the claim may not be honoured by the insurer, as the causes of death was not natural.

Medical Insurance/ Medical Aid Coverage

Medical aid cover is the fund you contribute into, monthly, to cover your general medical needs(such as visit to a doctor when you have further prescription for allergies, or medication or a birth of a baby at a hospital; whereas the Medical Insurance covers for certain expensive hospital procedures which the medical aid may not cover or when the medical aid funds have been exhausted, which may be a life threatening health situations such as cancer or heart attacks or serious car accident, but they happen without prior warning.

Endowment Policy

It is almost like a short term investment vehicle that can be used as a savings instrument with a specific term. It is usually used for example, deposit for a house, children's education or an overseas trip or in between jobs (if you are thinking of taking a break).

Company Group (Life Assurance)

This is inexpensive long term insurance life cover that is often taken up and paid for by the employer on behalf of employees; it pays out lump sum to the beneficiaries of members (employees after death); however unfortunately it is not transferable when you resign.

Company Disability Cover

The employer takes out disability cover for employee (member) insuring the members if they become disabled. If for any reason you are medically diagnosed with disability or terminal illness and cannot continue being competent in your duties, then the disability policy will pay out either monthly or a lump sum income to the employee (member) after it has been established and confirmed that the member is disabled.

Short term insurance includes motor vehicle insurance, home owner's insurance, household insurance, personal liability insurance, travel insurance, and business insurance.

Motor Vehicle insurance

When you buy a car, it is important, compulsory & necessary to take out an insurance to cover the debt and theft. If your car gets into accident or stolen and you're insured; your insurer will pay you out the value of the car as well as sometimes cover the debt to the bank and you can afford to buy another car (provided there is no balloon payment). Please check with your insurer. However, if you're not insured you would be in debt and with no car.

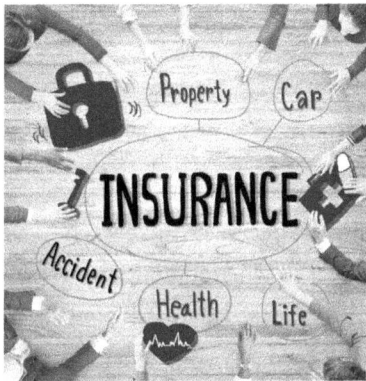

Household Insurance

God forbid this bad luck does not befall you, if a car drives through your house fence; or robbers cleans you out completely or the lightening strikes your house; so the household insurance will cover your loss and pay out the replacement value of the loss.

Home Owner's Insurance

If someone starts a fire by throwing the cigarette butts or by a bomb if in a war zone or by some natural disaster and your house catches fire and it burns down to ashes; you better make sure you have a home owner's insurance (compulsory if you have a bond with the bank) otherwise you will need to pray for a miracle, as you will need to have to dig deeper into your pockets to start all over again.

Personal Liability Insurance

This cover is against a party suing you (in your personal capacity) for financial loss experience as a result of physical injury or death or the financial loss could reach millions of Rands. It is not a necessity, however if you have it; you'll be grateful you did.

Travel Insurance

This short term insurance is required when you undertake an overseas trip and you're worried about your health or valuables, so it covers medical costs, loss of baggage, theft of valuables, even the loss caused by delays of flights.

Business Insurance

If an enraged employee working for a company next door to your company (in a block of offices) burns down the building or leaves a tap running over the week end, the business insurance should be used to cover most of the damage or even get to new premises and/or equipment. If there is no insurance or there is a limit to paid coverage, then your company will experience a huge set back and might not be able to return to normal operation.

Under and Over- Insurance

Under-insurance is where the sum insured is less than the amount of loss that the insured (you) would have suffered if the risk should materialize, remember the definition of insurance is where the insured takes out a cover to protect himself from an unforeseen life event (risk) for a certain specific amount with certain conditions, e.g. a property is insured for R450,000.00; however its market value is 550,000.00. An insured (you) may only recover the loss, i.e. R450,000.00 that was actually insured.

Over-Insurance

This occurs when the sum insured is greater than the loss that the insured would suffer if the risk materialize, e.g. a car is insured for R200,000.00, however its market value is R100,000.00, here in this example, the insured would not recover more than the actual loss he suffered; because the car loses (depreciates - as soon as it leaves the dealership) its value over time as compared to a house which appreciates in value over a period of time.

When choosing out insurance, take note of the following:

• Is the cover that you need (comfortable with the level of cover offered)?
• Can you afford the monthly premiums?
• Do you understand the terms and conditions of the policy (contract)?

IN CASES where there is an excess (payment that the insured must pay before the insurance company will pay out for the short term insurance claim; such as a car involved in a collision, it is damaged & needs repairs) that needs to be paid, does the insured know what it is and how much to be paid.

30 days cooling off period: This means you have 30 days to decide if you still interested in taking up the offer. If you do not need the policy anymore, you can cancel without paying except penalties applicable. If you cancel at any stage after 30 days, then you will be required to pay for the notice period (30 days/1 month) and other penalties may be applicable and payable.

When deciding to take out an insurance, you need to do an affordability calculation and needs analysis to establish if you need the cover and can afford the premiums.

Premiums refers to payments paid over to the insurance company which is usually monthly or yearly, but it is always paid in advance at the beginning of the month, e.g. pay 1 April, you are covered for April.

Beneficiaries are the person or people who will receive the benefit from your insurance policy/will.

Choose/nominate your beneficiaries/heirs of your estate in a will. Also note that an estate can take long to wind up. If you nominate beneficiaries on a policy they will receive the money (as it does not form part of the estate/assets).

When you choose children as beneficiaries, it may prove a challenge, particularly if they're below the age of 18 years and there is no guardian to handle this responsibility; eg. they will not be able to arrange for a funeral as adults would do. Make sure you choose a responsible, reliable, trustworthy guardian for your children who wants to take on that responsible role.

You can change or update your beneficiaries whenever a need arises or as often as you would like to (please check with your insurance company). Ensure that your policy is always up to date including beneficiaries; insurance companies have a duty to pay the correct person/people.

Paid Up Policy: The policyholder has paid for the cover in full and then dies. You find that there were dependents on that policy; so those dependents can still be covered by the original policy without paying any further premiums or alternatively can take out their own.

No claims benefit: This is a fully paid up, up-to-date policy but where you never made any claims on it at all, and some insurance companies reward people who do not claim by paying out bonuses, e.g. they will pay back all your premiums for certain time or you can claim a certain portion of your premiums at a certain age. Always ask or check with your insurance company for the details of the policy as they have different rules.

Waiting Periods: This refers to the time gap between when you take out the insurance policy and the activation of paying out at the time of claim; different policies have different waiting periods and in some cases there is no waiting period. Always, check with your insurance company for full details of the policy.

Exclusions: This is what the insurance company will not cover the risks involved and it helps the insurance companies to keep their premiums fair by removing certain risks. For example, in a life insurance, if you were to commit suicide or take yourself into a war zone; in the event of death, the insurer may not cover you; as the death did not happen as a result of natural causes.

It is important that you tell the truth when you take out the insurance. Should the insurance company finds out that you have been economical with the truth, they will not pay out anything or refuse to pay you out at all. They could cancel your insurance policy (contract) completely.

EIGHT

ROADMAP TO FINANCIAL WELLBEING - BUDGETING

A budget is telling your money where to go; instead of wondering where it went. - John C. Maxwell.

"I cheated on my fears, broke up with my doubts, engaged with my Faith, and now I am marrying my Dreams. The quality of your thinking determines the quality of your Life." - Bernard Shaw.

It begs the question of who is controlling your financial destiny? it is YOU. If you know where you are going, then you can reach your destination.

The Personal Spending Planner™ is a helpful tool that an individual can use to select:

• How to control and manage monthly expenses, savings, investments and debt

• Understand where all your Rands and Cents go?

• Help you save and invest for you & your loved one's financial future

• Getting out of excessive debt and build financial wealth and freedom.

Here is a kicker. We listen to the budget speech delivered by our esteemed Financial Minister twice, every year, yet we seldom put into practice and yet, we criticize that it does not work or it does not go far enough - it is precisely this lack of transparency & accountability that we avoid facing our own "demons"; if we don't, then who will? If we are expecting our government officials to be held accountable, transparent and deliver services to the various communities with diligence, should we not be the first to be held accountable to ourselves & loved one's and practise what we preach and expect? It makes you think, doesn't it?

Firstly, let us take a test to see if you are in control of your personal finances. Answer these questions with a Yes or a No.

1. I know and understand my pay slip.

2. I know exactly what I earn.

3. I know and understand the total amount of deductions on my pay slip.

4. I know how the UIF (Unemployment Insurance Fund) deduction is calculated.

5. I know and understand how my employer has calculated and deducted the correct amount of tax, medical aid, pension or provident fund.

6. I know and understand other non-obligatory ad hoc deductions, such as but not limited premium on policies, parking, canteen, union fees, garnishee order.

7. I know exactly how much money my employer pays over into my bank account.

8. I know and can track how much I spend each month.

9. I keep a record of my monthly expenses each month.

10. I know exactly how much money I owe each month.

11. I do my budget and try to stick to it each month.

Results based on the number of Yes answers

0-3 : No control over your personal finances.

4-7 : You show understanding. Needs improvement.

8-11: You're in full control. Keep it up and innovating.

NORMALLY, budget has a negative connotation as it creates stress and less confidence in handling personal finances; because if it does not work, it creates tension and resulting in failure.We have created the Personal Spending Planner™ that allows an individual to explore opportunities and possibilities, rather than limiting one to what is available. It splits the expenses, savings & investments, and debt into the following breakdown:

40% Fixed costs(household spent)
25% Financial services goals
10% Debt goals
25% Savings & Investments

To help minimize expenses (outflows) into few manageable categories that will allocate your paycheck easily. Work out how much you have (net salary) and then break down & work out:

• How much do you currently spend on household?
• How much of it you keep (savings & investments)?
• How much do you owe (debt)?
• How much do you save towards a financial goal (unpredictable & unplanned situations such as death, accident, medical expenses)?

When you work out how much you currently spend (household), owe (debt), use our Personal Spending Planner™ which includes:
• Fixed expenses (pay every month & regularly) e.g. rent, car, house payments.
• Variable expenses (pay every month but they change) e.g. groceries, electricity, transport).
• Irregular expenses (only happen every now & then) e.g. holiday, birthday, unplanned medical expenses.
• Include ALL your Debt in your Personal Spending Planner™.

Once the Personal Spending Planner™ is done, the bottom line will become clearly visible. Your balance books will either be positive (black) or negative (red). You'll have to face the facts. Be realistic about spending patterns and put plans in place to increase income or cut down on expenses to manage your debt. The goal is to balance the books back to a positive bottom line.

Budget Spending Tips

• Be realistic about your Personal Spending Planner™ (be more truthful & honest) about how much you earn, how much and where you select to spend and be disciplined about your spending patterns and your money.
• Differentiate and prioritize between needs and wants, so that you spend on necessary basic needs such as food & water, roof, basic health care & hygiene & clothes on your back (comfortable & appropriate dressing and not fancy popular brand bling bling names). Everything beyond this, a huge 4x4 or SUV (Sport Utility Vehicle) car or triple storey house, brand clothing names, fancy & expensive food & drinks is a "figment of our imagination" and let us be honest here, it is a want, because you cannot afford it, let alone maintain it.
• Impulsive or unplanned spending is driven by desires or wants or competition that only resides in our hearts and not our heads, these actions can have unintended spending consequences (constraints) that could arise as you sacrifice your basic needs for unnecessary wants. Thus, it is important to create well- thought-out steps to reach informed decisions.
• Review your spending patterns (ultimately balancing the books) as your needs and wants grow or change while going through life stages & ages of Life. Make it a habit to review your spending patterns on a fairly regular basis. Avoid costly

mistakes or surprises by keeping a record to ensure that your money went where you planned it to go.
• Forgive yourself. We are all human. You'll probably not get your books to balance as you planned the first time. Do not feel deprived or hold a grudge against yourself for not meeting your financial needs and goals. Do not give up the first time the planner fails as it will take time to create new spending habits. It is not a short term vacation around the harbour, it is a journey.

However, please do not misunderstand and misquote me. I do not mean that you must not or cannot enjoy Life. But Life must be lived within reason. Treat yourself kindly to the Life's indulgences and luxuries, but do it all in a way that you can AFFORD (within your means).

Benefits of Budgeting - Spending Patterns

• You can actually see in black and white how much or whether or not you spent more or less than what you earned.
• Having the Personal Spending Planner™ in front of you, helps you to realise almost immediately and identify what, how, where, with whom you're spending for and things you shouldn't be doing.
• It helps you get a better and clear overview and under-standing on how you are doing over time in the long run, as you can extend your columns in your spreadsheet to cover a year.
• By regularly looking at your Personal Spending Planner™, you get a sense of comfort and satisfaction that all that needs to be taken care of, has been taken care of - yours and your loved one's future; so you can plan with confidence.
• It helps everyone especially family members to come to the

same level of understanding because everyone is allowed to participate and be involved in the process of reaching an informed decision.

Creating a spending planner helps you get organized financially and assists in being prepared for what is going to be required to make it happen

As a final thought, see this as a new day, new beginning, second chance, an opportunity, to try again and see it as a valuable gift or lesson to be learnt and celebrate the milestones achieved thus far and possibilities to explore other options available and not see it as a curse, a grudge or a chore.

Company name	Royalty Pty Limited	Company Address	20 Royalty Street, Ark Palace, JHB, 2001	Payment Date: 25/02/2018
Employee code	0003210	Pay point	Johannesburg	Date engaged: 01/02/2015
Employee name	Zinzi Royalty Ark	Department	Sales & Marketing	Period: 12
		Job title	Sales Representative	Account #: 110001213143
Tax Reference	7771000000			Branch code: 25-06-08
				Leave Balance:5

Earnings			Deductions	
Basic Pay		R12054.10	PAYE	R3388.52
Travel Allowance		R1000.00	UIF	R135.54
Cellphone Allowance		R800.00	Medical Aid	R720.00
Total Earnings/ Gross Salary		R13554.10	Provident Fund	R550.00
			Loan/Advance	R400.00
			Total Deductions	R5341
			Net Salary	R8360.02

Sample Pay Slip

Employee code: This is the employee number or code allocated to you by the employer on joining the company.

Tax reference: This is the 10- digit tax reference number issued by SARS; either you or your employer would have registered you.

Basic Pay/cash earnings: This is an amount of salary paid to you before any additional benefits such as medical aid, pension/provident fund or allowance are added.Your basic salary is fixed every month and is taxable.

Taxable Income: This is the figure representing your income earned(usually after some deductions) that SARS uses to calculate the PAYE(Pay As You Earn) that your employer pays over to SARS automatically on your behalf.

UIF: This is a figure used to calculate your Unemployment Insurance Fund (UIF) contributions and is all income for employees with more than 24 hours pay in a month and excludes commission.Your employer will automatically calculate and deduct this amount from your gross salary and pay it over to UIF (Labour Department). As an employee, you pay 1% of your total salary and your employer pays another 1% of your salary to the fund every month. If you become unemployed after contributing to the UIF, you have the right to claim from the UIF. You will need to have been working at least 24 hours for the UIF to be deducted.

Payment date: This is the date on which your salary will be paid to you into your bank account.

Period: This is the tax month number(numbers 1-12) through out the tax year under review(March-February).

Account#: The banking account your salary will be paid into. Leave balance: This shows how many leave days are available to you currently.

PAYE: Pay As You Earn, your employer will deduct PAYE from your salary on a monthly basis and pay it over to SARS on your behalf. The amount of PAYE which you will contribute depends on how much you earn, and is calculated from tax tables issued yearly by SARS.

Net Salary: The amount that you take home after deductions such as UIF, PAYE, Medical Aid, Pension/Provident Fund have been paid by your employer. This is the amount that will appear in your bank account on the pay day.

Calculating Your Household Income

Monthly Household Income taking into account the deductions.

My Gross Salary		R13554.10
Tax(PAYE)	R3388.52	
UIF	R135.54	
Medical Aid Fund	R720.00	
Pension/Provident Fund	R550.00	
Other	R400.00	
Less: Total Deductions		(R5341.52)
My Net Income:		R8360.02

AS THE POPULAR SAYING GOES" You cannot effectively manage what you cannot measure", so to effectively manage and control your money(income) you need to be clear about what exactly is your household income. If you are single, then it will be a single income after tax & deductions. If you have a partner(spouse) your household income is a joint incomes(after taxes & deductions) of all the people sharing your household and the amount you have available for spending, saving and investing and debt.

When calculating household income, bear this in mind to include all other sources of income; e.g. your partner's income after tax & deductions, extra income for both such maintenance payments, child grants, disability payments, monthly pension, as rental income of lodgers(back room), part time job, sideline hobby/hustle business (eg.pap & vleis) at a soccer game, taxi, spaza shop (tuck shop); tell it all and everything. Using the sample payslip; you can then calculate your household income above.

Understanding and calculating Total Household Income process is essential, especially if the family is considering their financial future, savings, buying a car or a home or putting children through school or higher education or any other financial decision. If you would want to dive deeper you have the option of using our Personal Spending Planner™ to track your household expenses on a monthly basis, over a period of 12 months, to see how far you have come. At the end, it comes down to understanding and knowing (comfort) how much is coming in(inflows) and how much is going out(outflows) and how much is saved.

Expenses		Amount
Fixed Expenses		
Rent/Home loan		
Car Payments		
Personal Loan repayments		
Security		
Insurances		
School fees		
Garden services		
Home Cleaning services		
Other		
Total Fixed Expenses		= R
Variable Expenses		
Electricity & Water		
Pikitup		
Rates & Taxes		
Groceries		
Transport		
Entertainment		
Clothing account		
Toiletries/Cosmetics (hair, nails)		
Cellphone (voice/data bundles)		
Children miscellaneous		
Pet supplies		
Other		
Total Variable Expenses		=R
Irregular Expenses		
Medical Emergencies		
Household repairs		
Car Emergencies		
Gifts(house warm, baby showers, birthdays, dinner dates)		
Holiday expenses (Christmas, overseas trips, week end away)		
Pet Medical Emergencies		
Other (Festivals,parties, baby showers hosting)		
Other (Anniversary)		
Total irregular expenses		=R
Total Expenses		=R

In the final analysis it is not how much you earn, it is how much you get to keep, so that you can grow your wealth and experience financial freedom, so it is possible with financial astuteness and basic financial planning with discipline.

During our one-on-one mentorship session, we dive deeper using the Personal Spending Planner™ and we painstakingly go through each line item like a fine tooth comb to understand the background and the intentions of the spending pattern, as it will assist with the clarity of thought patterns, behaviour and financial wellbeing of the customer.

NINE

SAVINGS - SECURE YOUR GOALS, DREAMS & YOUR FUTURE

A journey of a 1000 miles,begins with one baby step at a time. I have added to it "that it opens up a new understanding, clarity, and following of one's Life meaning when you are deliberate about it. - Lao Tzu

---

We all dream of a better and great life for ourselves and our loved one's, one or some day in the future based on what we wish, we want, and we imagine our future to be. We should also bear in mind that, when it comes to your money, although you live in the present (now), the focus should be on how your money cannot only do now, but also stretch enough to focus on the future (dreams & goals) ensuring that some of it, is put away today so that it can work for your tomorrow.

It is also important to note that you must pay yourself first, before paying(sharing) your hard earned money with others, so that there's always enough to look after you when you really need it; it serves you like it should. Take it like a prepaid investment(paying forward before you need money) that would see your money grow and that will help you to achieve your goals, dreams and your future. What are we talking about, I will tell you what we are talking about, savings and investments, being frugal and smart about how to spend your hard earned money wisely. When we do not save or invest, we are basically "robbing and stealing from our future" and that of our loved one's and that my friend is the most horrific injustice we can ever commit to ourselves and our beloved ones.

Why do we need to save, so we're saying when you're daydreaming about your future, do bear in mind that those dreams, goals require money; so the question is, where will that money come from? Lottery, gambling or a get-rich-quick-scheme are not the answer, hey some of us are not lucky, where some lost relative leaves us with some huge inheritance; we have to work, good luck if you have won the Lotto (hope and pray that you have used it wisely).

What are your goals? What needs might you be saving for?

• Do you want to buy your own car, how much will it cost you, bearing in mind that the bigger the car, the most expensive, remember needs vs wants.
• What kind of education do you want for your children and

perhaps improvement of your own. What will it cost you, considering that education is the best investment (gift) that you can give to your children and yourself.

• You cannot really know in advance when will you need that extra money, especially during unforeseen events (sudden loss of a job or income, children getting sick, major operation) and Life stages (ages and stages) that sometimes throws us off when we were didn't see it coming, so by creating an extra pad (Emergency Fund) to cushion the impact that "seem" to happen spontaneously or at random; so what would it cost you to survive the tough times, until your recover.

• Have you dreamt of taking a dream holiday one day overseas before you kick the bucket (before you die) and how much will this trip cost (set you back)?

I trust that you realize that it is important to save for those unforeseen random situations!

Types of Savings Vehicles (list not exhaustive)
• Money box (Mattress) shoe/pig money box
• Savings club
• Savings account
• Stokvel
• Tax free savings account
• Notice deposit (32 days, 7 days notice account)
• Call account
• Fixed deposit

How to Save

17 Practical Life-Changing Strategies that you can start using today.

1. Make savings fun: Create a fun competition within family members or friends to keep the momentum going and lasting (stick to it).

2. Look into saving on bank charges and insurance: Keep reviewing how much it costs you, to have and keep the bank account you hold and insurance(contract terms and conditions).

3. Buy what you need: Plan and only buy food that you really to avoid waste.

4. Buy in bulk: This helps to save in the long run, especially goods with long shelf life like toilet paper, washing powder, dish- washing liquid and washing powder.

5. Avoid buying convenience food: How much would you save if you cooked food at home and also consider preparing fresh ingredients that will enhance your lifestyle as you can control both costs and what goes into your body.

6. Take a lunchbox to work: Take leftover meals to work to avoid unnecessary spending. Doing this forces you to be realistic about your money and helps with your priorities. Let me help show you what I mean. Let's say you spend R30,00 for a plate of pap and meat at Tshisanyama (Food truck) everyday. That works to R150,00 per week. Spent over over 49 weeks, it comes to R7350,00. That's an amount you could be saving by

bringing a lunchbox to work instead. It makes sense to prioritize your spending habits.

7. Eat before you go out for shopping: This goes for children too, as well as adults, because you spend more money when you're hungry(to fill the void) instead when you're full you tend to be more careful.

8. Make a shopping list of the required items and stick to it even if there's ongoing specials (if it is not on the list, ignore/avoid, move right along).

9. Compare prices: We live in an internet age (information is freely available) so it has made our lives easier to compare and save time, e.g. update and review needs (cellphone packages)

10. Do not be a slave to retail therapy: It has its good and bad ways; delay the immediate (instant gratification) by buying on impulse, take time to do research, compare prices/items, read reviews of what other people think of the use of the items, consider all available options before committing your hard earned cash about a purchase especially big ticket items such as fancy car, expensive furniture, latest fashion fad, bling items. Stop being a fashion victim. Be a financial winner.

11. Use electricity sparingly: Switch off lights in rooms that are not occupied, so it goes for appliance as well - saves energy and lasts longer, use light bulbs and appliance that are energy efficient.

12. Be smart in how and when to shop: Familiarize yourself with seasonal sales, e.g. buy your clothes when season changes (at the end of winter buy winter fashion clothing that is when

retail shops get rid of their stocks to make way for summer, so at the end of summer you buy summer clothes. In this way, you buy good quality, long-lasting clothing at reduced prices.

13. Avoid swiping your plastic card: It is too easy and convenient to use our credit, cheque and debit cards as there no charges when you use them. We do not stop to think that when we use the card the same amount leaves the bank account. You wonder what happened to your money? Instead, withdraw enough cash to pay the bill. You will also save on bank charges and interest. It psychologically registers how much you are withdrawing. Keeping receipts helps you track your overall spending and keep to a budget.

14. Work together as a team (family, partnership): There is no point in trying to save, in a case where there's no communication within the family structure(get buy-in from family members) to gain support and working together; this is a recipe for financial victory. The benefit is that you can always hold each other accountable when not sticking to plan.

15. Check your budget and track your money regularly: Continuously review your budget (keep receipts, check your transactions online, update your budget as regularly as is possible weekly, monthly, quarterly) checking spending vs earnings; keep on cutting costs, spending less and save money.

Once you get comfortable in repeating these steps, soon you'll be in a place where you start building wealth and the next step (big question) is what you are going to do with the money you saved? Maybe reward yourself and take that long overdue vacation you promised (dreamt) for yourself.

16. Change your habits, change your lifestyle: Imagine having a clean bill of health, healthy bank balance, this is what smokers realise when they quit smoking that they can save between R50,00 - R80,00 each time on a packet of cigarettes. Imagine that adding up to an amazing incredible saving each month and even more in a year.

17. Find your own suitable saving amount: Try and aim to save an amount each month - usually 10% is a reasonable start. If you earn R6000,00, then you should save R600,00; but if it feels like it is too much, then start with what you can afford to save and put away every month. The popular saying goes that it is better to start small than to procrastinate or to never to start at all. Once you have decided on an amount, then create a stop order from your bank account to allow your money to be deducted automatically, to a separated savings account to avoid the temptation to have an excuse of not saving.

TEN

INVESTMENT - HOW TO MAKE YOUR MONEY GROW (COMPOUNDING GROWTH INTEREST)

Compound interest is the eighth wonder of the world. He who understands it, earns it... he who doesn't.... well pays it. - Albert Einstein.

When you save and invest, you are using your initial money to make you more money and making it grow by itself (make money work for you and we call it compounding growth which means that you're making money on your original investment and on the gains (interest earned) in the years to come and if you leave the investment untouched (without withdrawing) for long periods of time; the investment grows each year and exponentially because, of compound interest effect. If you understand the compound interest principle and its workings, then you'll appreciate the most powerful and awesome tool that you possess that would help you build wealth over time and leave a legacy for your loved ones.

Differentiate between savings and investing

Savings refers to monthly deposits into a low risk savings account that gives an individual an opportunity to save money and grow (it is on the interest earned basis therefore the funds must be easily accessible and available on demand) and liquid cash(available funds held on hand). It is usually for a short term goal (less than a year) and/or for an unexpected spontaneous event that normally happens on a person's life unannounced/uninvited).

ON THE OTHER HAND, the main purpose of investments is to build sustainable, steady, continuous flow of wealth which over a long period of time will realise huge returns on investment. It is advisable not to withdraw/touch the investment during its growing period, otherwise, it will not yield the desired and expected results.

Investment vehicles that you can consider:
- Government Bonds
- Unit trusts
- Shares/Equity in public listed companies

- Bonds
- Retirement Annuities (RA)
- Pension Fund
- Provident fund
- Endowment Policy

What are your goals - different needs that you might be investing for:

- Grow your money. Investing your money can allow you to grow it. ...
- Save for retirement, as you would like to maintain the same lifestyle after retirement and not rely on your family or Government pension to take care of you.
- Earn higher returns.
- Reach financial goal
- Start and expand a business.
- Support others.

4 Benefits of Investing

- You Stay Ahead of Inflation. If you don't invest and grow your money, you'll actually end up losing money over time
- It will help you build wealth smartly.
- Investing will get you to Retirement (Or Early Retirement) comfortably
- Other investments vehicles such property can help you save on taxes.

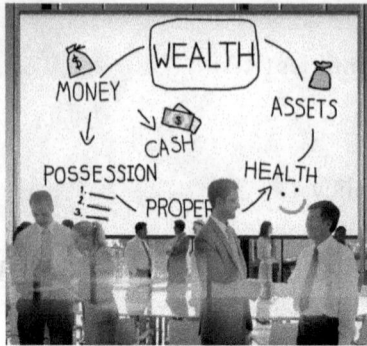

Comparison of Interest Earned with Simple Interest vs Compound Interest

Simple interest is an additional amount earned (profits on investing and leaving your money with the bank/financial institution for saving your money in other saving vehicle. Simple interest calculation, this is an additional amount (initial deposit/initial investment) paid into the low risk savings account vehicle and on the other hand simple interest is the additional cost paid/charged on the original amount borrowed (principal paid/charged) on the original amount borrowed (principal amount) and not on the interest owed on the loan. Whereas,

Compound interest refers to when interest is added to an original investment amount and the interest that has been added also earns more interest (earning interest on interest) and usually calculated daily, but credited daily, monthly, quarterly, semi-annually or annually depending on how the investment is structured such as, a Call account or 12 month fixed investment, on both the principal (original investment) and the credited interest.

Let's look at an example (scenario) to illustrate the interest calculation with simple interest; let's say your granny has been savings R500,00 every month for 12 months and she kept her savings in a pantyhose under the mattress (do not laugh, that is what our African grannies did back in the day). At the end of 12 months, she had accumulated R6000,00. However had she taken that money and saved it into a low risk savings account in a bank, she would benefit by being paid a fixed % of every Rand invested in the savings account, because the risk of a savings account is low, the returns are also low.

The benefit for the granny is that the savings account offers her safety (unlike in her house where her money may run the risk of being stolen, lost or destroyed by fire) and guaranteed interest paid by the bank. Please bear in mind that the real value of the savings will be less, considering the reality of inflation which eats away on the initial value of money over time.

Let us look at how to calculate simple interest on savings. The equation to calculate is:

Principal X Interest rate X time

Let us say we take granny's R6000.00 that she earned over 12 months at a simple interest rate of 6,5% per year, and would like to know how much interest you would earn;

P x R x T = interest
R6000,00 X 0,065 X 12 = R390
After 12 months, she would have R6390. back with simple interest calculation

Now that we have understood the basic simple interest calculation; we now need to understand the complex compound interest calculation; although it is important for you to grasp the calculation, you do not need to carry a scientific calculator around to work out the interest, both the banks and financial institutions can do the calculation for you, so you can breathe a sigh of relief.

Let us look at the compound interest formula:

P = I (1 + interest/compounded over time monthly; yearly; quarterly) months x compound years (to the power of)

It does look very complicated; luckily you do not need to calculate it yourself, the bank usually does; however it is very easy to calculate, if you have all the information; let's say you want to invest R2000,00 over 12 years, compounded monthly at a rate of 10% per annum, you would get R6607,30 at the end of 12 years.

$$2000(1+0,10/12)(12x12)144 = R6607,30$$

The wonderful and great news about using this compounded growth tool is that you have to save over a long period of time, for it to work effectively, it is important to start investing early so you can take advantage of time; if you delay the process of starting then you're stealing from your future and that of your loved one and from reaching your financial goals of taking advantage of the compounded interest earnings. It does not matter where you are at right now; the good news is that you can always start to invest small regular amounts until you can graduate to lump sum investments - so it is never too late to START and you can start today.

Consider the following investments strategy tips
• Identify what you are saving for
• Determine how much you can start with
• Choose appropriate solutions/vehicles that work for you(risk appetite)

• Make it automatic, so you forget it
• Monitor your progress (Celebrate milestones reached)

---

13 Strategies for Successful Investing

If you want to invest, you should first get your financial house in order to avoid chaos. You can turn to Chapter 8 "The Roadmap to Financial Wellbeing" and Chapter 11-13 to learn how to manage debt.

I would like to assume that I speak for all of us, that we would like to live a fantabulous comfortable life at retirement age. Planning for that comfortable, stress free, retirement days, is a long term journey (process) that requires patience, empowerment, effort, carefully well thought out plans (series of decisions). There is a pearl of wisdom that reads "Rome was never built in one day", so it requires patience and knowledge and not a sail around the harbour and true wealth was never built overnight. Before considering various and sometimes confusing investment options, you need to equip yourself by conducting information gathering exercise(desktop research) and understanding of the important secrets(strategies) for successful investing such as:

"Eat First" = "Invest in yourself first before you spend": Pay yourself first by securing and protecting you and your family's future (emergencies) in times of need. It means that when you receive your salary, you should slice it into different portions i.e. save some, spend some and pay over what you owe (in that chronological order).

Start Early: By starting early, it gives you an opportunity(advantage) to earn the benefits of compounded interest & growth on your investments and allows you to make mistakes and earn while doing it. It is never too late to start, the only difference will be your strategy and risk appetite(do you possess a low/safe, medium or high returns personality drive).

Consider the Risk of Your Investment: Understand that the risk affect the returns & growth capability of your investments and that is why it is important to conduct that research to get to understand what kind of an investor you are. Higher returns means greater risks, so be prepared to lose harder and greater, so it is better to choose a risk level that you are comfortable with, that you can afford emotionally (tolerate) and financially (risk gaining or losing). Your risk should consider and perhaps to a greater extent to suite your income, family situation and life stages and age.

Look at the Bigger Picture: It is important to do your homework before you invest, understand your financial situation and how the chosen investment fit into your lifestyle; also examine your debt burden, tax situation, ability to fund retirement account and insurance coverage.

Avoid Get-Rich-Quick Schemes: If it sounds too good to be true, it probably is and remember this, true wealth is built over time, through long term investment and patience and NOT OVERNIGHT.

Think Long Term (Have a long term strategy): Make up your mind and keep it set on the selected good investment and hold it for a long stretch and do not chop and change, often, when the market is not delivering the result you expect, over a short period of time; even the best performing investments go through good and difficult or tough (high and lows) periods. Changing investment may be expensive and also you lose out on potential earnings (compounded interest) while in depressed period. Many investments only show real growth after long period of time, e.g. 5- 10 years.

Do Not Put Your Eggs in One Basket (Diversify your portfolio): You should hold a variety of investments (make sure you have a range of low, medium and high risk investments); this allows you to be cushioned when something goes wrong, e.g. should you choose to invest in unit trusts, cash, real estate (property), shares (equity/stocks), invest both locally and globally as well, so that if the local market is down, you can gain in the global market and vice versa. Speak to your Financial Planner.

Minimize fees: Ask to see the breakdown of all administration costs, broker's fee and commission upfront, before signing any policy or investment, to see how much of your investment goes to cover administration costs and how much is actually invested because, the more you pay in commissions and management fees, on your investment, the longer it takes for the returns to be earned.

Past Performance is No Indication (Guarantee) of Future Performance: Like life, investments are also unpredictable; it does not mean that if an investment has done exceptionally well in the past; it could just as well continue as such in the future; it all depends on so many factors such as, the market performance, the economic environment, management strategy and sentiment, tax regime, inflation (as it eats away into your investment growth potential).

Take Tax Regime into Account: Take advantage of tax deductible retirement/savings account and also, educate and understand the impact of taxes on your investments and speak to your financial advisor about adapting your investment portfolio, to keep it balanced and to meet the needs of changing times and environment.

Preserve your Pension/Provident Fund (Savings): When you move in between jobs, do not be tempted to cash out, otherwise, the taxman will be ready to pounce on your hard earned cash over the years (end up paying unnecessary & more taxes) and you lose out on the effects of compounding interest, so preserve, preserve, preserve your savings as much as is possible!

Review Your Investments Regularly: Read actively all statements carefully and be on top of your game (understanding) and check your returns.

Save Your Family Grief By Getting Independent Financial Advice

Some people have the misconception that you only need independent financial advice if you are wealthy, but that is not the case. The job of a financial advisor is to help you protect and grow your money, whether you have a lot of money or a small amount of money to begin with. An advisor can help you to minimize your tax costs, choose the right life insurance, investments and plan your estate. So financial advisors are not only for the rich, but they can help anyone to work towards achieving their financial goals.

Some financial advisors are better than others so don't just settle for the first one you come across. Here are a few guidelines that can help you to find the best independent financial advisor.

1. You want to find out a little about the advisor, such as what credentials do they have? Are they an independent advisor or a tied advisor? How long have they been in the financial advisor profession? You want to look for someone with the right qualifications and that has the experience to know what they are doing.

2. You want an advisor that listens to what you are saying and takes your opinions into consideration when making your finance plan. This is your money that they are giving advice on so you want to have some say in what you do. A good advisor will listen to you, learn your needs and your financial situation and then find the best product or service to suit your needs. If an advisor is rushing you because he has another appointment following or if he doesn't explain things clearly, then you might be better off finding someone else.

3. You want an advisor that is reasonably flexible and willing to meet with you on a regular basis. You will need to remember that the advisor will have other clients so you don't want to abuse his services, but a good agent will meet with you as often as needed to keep your finances in order. This is particularly important if something unexpected comes up like a death in the family or a birth of a child, or loss of a job these situations may

require an earlier than expected meeting with your financial advisor.

4. Sometimes it is just about how you feel about the financial advisor. You may get a good or bad vibe with them and if you are not comfortable with them then don't hire them. You want someone that you like, someone that you feel comfortable with and someone that you feel confident for them to handle your finances. You don't want to hire someone that you are not comfortable with or just have a bad feeling about. Trust your instincts and only hire someone you like.

5. Self Empowerment through knowledge & information allows you to have power, control and also helps you evaluate the competence of those whom you hire, to understand your own needs and make sure that the advice you get, is valuable, accurate and comes from a good sincere heart and that proper needs analysis is conducted by your advisor to confirm your intention and in line with your financial planning goals. Ask as many questions, if you do not understand.

This is your money, your future and a good financial advisor will always remember that. They will work for you and in your best interest. If they can't do that to your satisfaction then you need to find someone who can. If an advisor is only interested in selling you a product or service, but not interested in getting to know your needs, then find someone who can and will.

These guidelines should help you to find a good independent financial advisor that will help you to make the most of your finances and achieve your financial goals.

ELEVEN

WHAT IS DEBT?

The are two kinds of people, those who earn interest
and others who pay it, unfortunately those who pay it,
do not understand the value of it, because they are
ignorant. - Albert Einstein

Debt can be briefly described as " draining your wealth; stealing
from yourself, your future, your loved one's, so tread carefully
before taking on debt.

Do you know how much it costs to borrow money from a
bank or financial institution, furthermore how much it costs
you to maintain the debt load for the period specified especially
when interest rates increases. There are two kinds of people.
Those who earn interest and others who pay it. Unfortunately,
those who pay it do not understand the value of it because they
are ignorant. Are you also aware that debt steals away from you
and your family's future?

Debt is an agreement (arrangement) contract entered into by a consumer and a financial institutions such as banks or micro lenders in order for the consumer to receive funds NOW. This debt must be repaid later, within a stipulated date; which is usually accompanied by a charge (initiation fee, administration fee, interest fee). These paybacks are arranged via debit order, cash payment, salary deduction.

Understanding the Types of Debt
• Secured Debt: It is where the creditor guarantees that the asset will be paid back unless you use an asset you own as a guarantee called a lien; if consumer does not pay, then the creditor can take the asset away.
• Unsecured Debt: This is where the consumer takes out credit by simply giving an oath or your promise or your word that the (you) consumer will pay back what has been lent out by the creditor.
• Healthy Debt: The key word is AFFORDABILITY, so that if the consumer can afford and pay it and where it can enhance (improve) one's situation (financial or life) then it is healthy debt, e.g. education loan to study further, home loan (asset increase in value and also provide shelter).

• Unhealthy Debt: This is the debt that is taken which worsens the financial situation and the debtor lives beyond their means. The debt becomes so negative that the consumer cannot pay it back and it lowers their credit score. When the consumer borrows from unregistered, unregulated micro lenders, they are charged large amount of interest.

Be aware before you take on or out debt. Shop around and do a comparison among financial institutions to see who charges more or less interest (cost) in line with one's needs for the loan (credit). Most of these institutions have a loan calculator.

Be careful again to stick to the amount you need and not be tempted and get excited by a lending consultant who wants to sell you more (remember it is their job to sell) than what you need, as it has an effect on your repayment of that loan and interest implications.

Take to heart the cost to maintain that debt for the period specified, as you imagine interest rates (cost) go up and down, so if it goes up, will the consumer be able keep up (maintain) the repayments?

Before taking up that credit card or personal loan, have you exhausted all avenues (researched the meeting of your needs), for example can the consumer not perhaps delay the purchase or save and buy later or use own savings to purchase the items, as this may save the consumer exorbitant related costs, interest rates, so taking out a loan should be the last resort.

Nowadays, we also have gone back to a layaway (lay-by) system (by the way, this system was used during the Apartheid era), where one pays a 10% deposit of the original amount for the goods, (it was popular in the clothing Retail space) then pay the remainder by 6 installments until paid in full. In a bit of good news it does not accrue any interest. This method was used by our grandparents (ancestors) who did not earn so much money at the time and they survived. They were neither in debt or were over-indebted. They were very disciplined and fearful of debt.

Do you understand what and how much it costs you to borrow (do the calculations on personal loans, overdraft, car)?

On successful application, a lender or credit provider will grant you credit or a loan which must be paid back over the period of time agreed upon and with interest for holding that money in use.

Always choose a loan repayment (installment) that suits you and your pocket (affordability), your needs and choose a period that will suit your financial situation. Bearing in mind that the monthly repayments will have statutory value on them such as a compulsory service or administration fee, credit life which varies from various financial institutions and the size of the debt and finally an initiation fee.

Let us use the example below to explain how it works. This depends on your credit profile, the prevailing rates and personal circumstances.

How much does a loan actually cost you on a R4000,00 loan?

Total repayments over 2 years (24 months) =@ 10% R800 per month X 24 = R19,200.

Total interest over 2 years = R15,200 (R19,200 - R4000)

Total repayments over 3 years(36 months) = @ 10% R1,200 per month X 36 = R43,200. Total interest over 3 years = R39,200 (R43,200 - R4000)

Total repayments over 5 years(60 months) = @ 10% R2000 per month X 60 = R120,000 Total interest over 5 years = R 116,000 (R120,000 - R4000)

Let us look when you take out a R10,000 loan.

Total repayments over 2 years(24 months) = 10% @ R2000 per month X 24 = R48,000.Total interest over 2 years = R38,000(R48,000 - R10,000)

Total repayments over 3 years (36 months) = @ 10% R3000 per month X 36 = R108,000.Total interest over 3 years = R98,000(R108,000 - R10,000)

Total repayments over 5 years (60 months) = @ 10% R5000 per month X 60 = R300,000.Total interest over 5 years (60 months) = R290,000(R300,00 - R10,000)

If you borrowed R25,000 loan, what would it cost you?

Total repayments over 2 years (24 months) = @ 10% R5000 per month X 24 = R120,000.Total interest over 2 years = R95,000 (R120,000 - R25,000)

Total repayments over 3 years (36 months) = @ 10% R7500 per month X 36 = R270,000. Total interest over 3 years = R245,000 (R270,000 - R 25,000)

Total repayments over 5 years (60 months) = @ 10% R 12,500 per month X 60 =R750,000. Total interest over 5 years = R725,000 (R750, 000 - R25,000)

What do you begin to notice?

• When you calculate the total interest charged, a picture begins to emerge where it becomes clear how much interest is being charged over different time periods.

• It is clear from this table that it is better to repay loans over a shorter period and alt-hough the monthly installments seem cheaper, if you take out a loan over a longer period; the total amount paid back is far much more in some cases it is 30 times

more than the amount of loan you initially requested &
taken out.

• The lender does not always specify the interest rate. If they
had told you, you would not have taken out the loan in the first
place, or you would have to think it over (sleep over it thus
delaying in taking out the loan). They are hoping that you will
remain ignorant and not do the calculations. Please be warned.
Read the fine (small) print as it never states the actual rates
used. It all depends on your personal circumstances.

• There is always a warning that the rates are subject to change,
so you may find yourself paying higher monthly installments if
rates were to increase without you knowing.

• There are also other costs to consider such as initiation fee,
administration fee, credit life insurance (e.g. short term insurance on a car purchase price a well as the person taking out the
loan, if there is no life cover supporting the loan) which may be
low, but over time may add up, which will definitely increase
the size of the loan you originally negotiated.

The National Credit Regulator (NCR) came into effect back in June 2007 to put in place:

• Rules and regulations for consumers and credit providers.

• Credit Providers requests credit agencies such as credit
bureaus for a consumer's credit report so that they can offer
credit based on the consumer's valid, accurate and correct
credit historical behaviour, as reflected on the credit report (it is
also the consumer's primary responsibility to ensure that their
own credit records are accurate and valid). Read the chapter 20
on Understanding & protecting your credit score - credit rating.

• The Act also limits credit providers from offering loans/credit
that the consumer can-not afford (reckless lending).

• The Act also sets limits on interest rate, the credit providers can charge consumers, so that consumers can be protected and avoid being taken advantage of.

Please take greater care when shopping, or intending to take out loans and it is a good idea to shop around for the best, cost effective credit provider, as they are competing for your business. Once again, ASK if you do not understand.

TWELVE

BAD DEBT VS GOOD DEBT

All worthwhile people have good thoughts, good ideas and good intentions, but precious few of them ever translate those into action. - John Hancock

---

Good Debt

These key questions are essential to whatever you call it resolutions, setting goals, reaching your objectives, meeting your needs carefully and purposefully, which will lead to deliberate planning and action and to do that is you have to ask the following questions:

Is it affordable, is it an investment towards your financial future, does it have a positive impact in your overall financial position, e.g. home loan (it appreciates in value) student loan (offers an opportunity to improve life's circumstances in the long term) buying a car that you can afford (has a realistic affordable repayment plan including interest rate increases)?

Bad Debt

The critical questions to ask is it draining your wealth, health, weighing your spirit down, can you afford it, does it offer real prospect of paying for itself in the future, e.g borrowing money to pay food, for instance, using store credit cards to pay for food at ridiculously high interest rates; buying a brand new car on residual (balloon payment) that you think you can afford, but in reality you cannot; luxurious holiday paid on credit card you cannot afford.

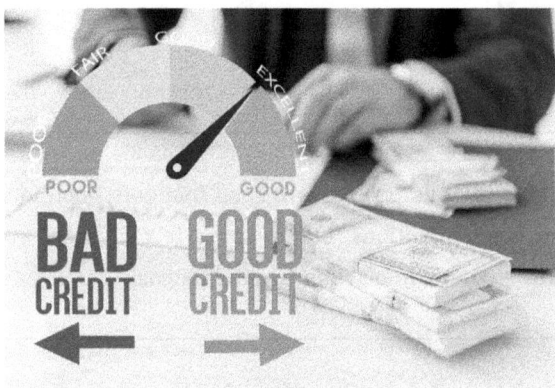

Here are some of the questions (checklist) that can help you to "test the waters" before taking action (on debt):
• Do I need this loan right now or can I postpone (hold off for now) this action for later or can I use my own funds for this?
• Have I shopped around to get the best deal in town?
• Am I borrowing this money as cheaply as is possible?
• Will I be able to cope (maintain) with the monthly install-ments should interest rate rise in future?
• Do I understand ALL the terms and conditions (include the small fine print) associated with borrowing this money?

• Do I understand ALL the risks and what could happen, if things go wrong?

If any of the answers are honestly responded to with mostly 'NO' then you would be most likely be realistic about understanding good vs bad debt and your current situation. We would encourage that you take the necessary steps as addressed in those questions as they would provide a great guide to taking responsible action and reaching a comfortable, satisfactory & rational informed decision.

Debt to Income Ratio

MANAGING and controlling your debt displays the most financial responsibility that you have towards yourself, your loved one's and your financial planning. It is always a good idea to figure out how much debt/load you have and compare to how much you earn and another way to look at it, is how much of your take home is used to pay off your debt. This exercise will help gain an understanding of your financial standing (health gauge).

Let us work out a debt-to-income ratio (debt load) which means how much debt is used up by the take home income earned. Debt load is the total sum of all the monies owed by you to your creditors whether calculated monthly or total amount owing so that you have a clear sight or view of where you stand.

Total monthly debt is equal to R11 500.00 and monthly take home pay(earnings after tax deductions - net pay) is equal to R15 000.00, i.e. ratio is equal to (debt divided by income x 100 = 77%).

It means that, more than half of your salary goes to pay debt, and the question is what do you live on, and that is why it leads to living on credit(personal loans, credit cards, overdraft, micro lenders loans) to survive the next month, and the following months, until you cannot live anymore, which at first leads to denial, then guilt, then stress, then depression and finally suicidal thoughts.

If the ratio is between 0-30%, your debt-to-income ratio is still acceptable/reasonable and it is still under control and you are responsible and managing for your income (money)

If the ratio is above 40%-50%, your debt gauge indicate a red flag and needs immediate and urgent remedial action, otherwise danger zone(financial demise/disaster which is above 70%) will be declared on you and would spiral into serious difficulty where possibly we can call you bankrupt/declared sequestrated case

If we look at the calculation above, it will most likely result in creditors turning their backs on you and be less likely open to extend any credit/loan to you or mostly likely charge you exorbitant (high) interest rate.

Your Credit Score - Do's And Don'ts

ANYBODY WHO IS FINANCIALLY aware has heard of a credit score and understands that it's better to have a higher one as opposed to a lower one. Lenders, employers, landlords, and others may look at your credit score before deciding whether or not to continue doing business. Now that's an important number! Think about it, if your credit score is too low you may not be able to get a loan, the job you want or live in the home of your choice.

Credit scores are determined using different criteria. It basically comes down to how much you earn, how much you owe and when you pay your bills. For example, if you are late paying your telephone/cellphone bill, your phone company may report it to any combination of the three main credit reporting agencies (not all creditors report to the same agencies). When this happens, you will get a mark against you on your credit report. And this, in turn, has a negative impact on your creditworthiness.

However, there are other things that can count against you, such as:

- Having too many credit accounts at any one time.
- Closing accounts that have a remaining balance on them.
- Too many open accounts, regardless of whether or not they have a balance.
- Lack of a credit history, especially when starting out in a new job
- Total outstanding debt that is too high.
- Having administration or sequestration order (bankruptcy) on your record.
- Not making payments on time.
- Not enough of a credit history.
- Having too much debt for your income (commonly referred to as high debt-to-income ratio).
- Closing too many accounts within a short time frame.
- Unpaid/delayed bills.

Each of the above things can raise a red flag on your credit report. How much any single one of these affects your credit score is hard to say, as each agency uses a different formula for calculating their score. At the very least, the things on the list don't look good. The more things you are doing on the list, the worse your credit score will suffer.

Now that we have listed things to avoid out of the way, it's time to get proactive. The good news is that there are things you can do that have a positive effect on your credit score. On top of that, they will also save you money in the long run and improve your overall state of financial health.

Only apply for credit when you need it, and do your best to space out when you apply for new credit accounts.
- Buy things with cash instead of credit.
- Stick to a budget so you don't spend more than you earn.
- Pay more than the minimum due on your credit cards.

- Build up a savings account so you have money for emergencies.
- Check your credit report for accuracy and make corrections where needed.
- Pay all of your bills on time.
- Correct errors on your report promptly.

Credit Repair Secret Tips To Help You

Most people don't realize it but there are actually several credit repair secret tips that you can use to help undo the damage that's been done to your credit score. None of this information is widely advertised, I mean, why would it be? An uninformed consumer is a sitting duck to all the threats and harassment of creditors. Don't ever forget though, that you do have rights and that debt collectors (creditors) have strict rules they have to follow.

The first thing you want to do is make sure that whatever negative things are on your credit report are accurate. It's important to check your credit reports from all three most popular credit bureaus, at least once a year and it is FREE. If you find a mistake, contact the credit bureau immediately in writing and request that it gets corrected. This simple tip can help you raise your score and get rid of inaccurate information that has been costing you money in higher interest rates.

When you contact a credit bureau keep a detailed file as to the date you sent the letter, sending it certified or registered mail may be a good idea, as well as a copy of the letter you sent them. Unfortunately sometimes the credit bureau isn't right on top of everything. It's a good idea that you keep track of everything in case they try to jerk you around.

When you are requesting that something gets changed or corrected you don't have to be timid. Don't treat them like you are a servant requesting a favor. Of course you want to be polite and professional but you aren't asking them for a favor you are asking them to correct a mistake. Don't let them push you around.

Don't expect this process to happen quickly. By law, the credit bureau has up to from 30-45 days to get back to you but sometimes it can take much longer. This is a process and you have to let the process work it's way out no matter how long it takes and how aggravating it can be.

If you want to work on your credit because you are contemplating buying a new home or car and you want to get approved, don't wait until the last minute. Start right now on repairing your credit. Remember, this is a process and it will take time.

While you are waiting for the process to work, make sure that you make all your payments on time. That includes all your household bills such as cellphone contract, store cards, electric (power) bills and not just your loan payments. You may not realize it but all companies that you have credit with, can report you to the credit bureaus too and late payments can affect your credit score.

You can rebuild your credit without resorting to underhanded tactics if you're willing to devote the time and consistency it will take and that may well be the biggest credit repair secret of all. Don't forget, the sooner you get started, the sooner you'll qualify for a great rate on that new car loan or mortgage, and that will be great!

THIRTEEN

GET OUT OF DEBT - VOLUNTARY PLAN

Get out debt quickly and permanently (for all time), others call it to lose your debt obligation, dump the loan obligation load, some call it management of debt obligation, others call it to dispose off the obligation. These terms mean something very similar and you need to get the correct attitude, build up another behavior to set the pace to take up the best possible position that forces an ultimate goal – money related principles, budgetary freedom, monetary prosperity.

We as a whole are mindful that it is difficult from the beginning, however possible if followed with vigor, making little strides will eventually lead to a positive outcome. Today, I will give you supportive step by step trips, hacks, insider secrets and habits (changed conduct) that you can use right now to address the elephant in the room.

"Your giant, your obstacle, your problem is a gateway to your significance and promotion" – Rick Godwin

I have accumulated 9 tricks, hacks, and insider facts that you can begin doing right now to get-out- debt quickly and permanently.

• **Give us a chance to hold an open, fair, straight-forward yet hold a conscious genuine discussion.** First things list all your debts (who, how much, for what, where and at what loan interest rate fee). Separate it into least install-ments expected for each and every account known to you – no omission. Try not to freeze at this stage, you are simply taking an inventory (stock) of the present situation of every one of your obligations and simply wonder about it, for you to have a reasonable picture – not focusing at past thoughts or mistakes. You are focussing on where you are going – what's to come.

• **Everything begins with your psyche.** Remember any best-lasting habit to shape in your brain, you need to make habits that change over your behavior, so start with "All is working out for me, even though I don't see any changes right now, everything is working out for me – repeat it again and again and state it all the time you feel overpowered and scared. Think about these words taking shape in your mind, breathing out stress & strongholds that have grasped and held you prisoner for a long time. Along these lines, we state, what would I like to get out of this, at the end of the day, what is the ultimate goal – to be free from these obligations and create lasting experience money related opportunity. The picture will be actually quite difficult, however, you need to concentrate on the main job and start finding a way, to gather speed, when you get moving you are gradually cutting off the dread of paralysis, best accept that interruption will raise its ugly ears, yet simply continue reminding yourself WHY you do this, as it will keep you focussed on a definitive reward (solution), as opposed to the issue, regardless of whether you don't see the results immediately, don't give up, simply continue onward.

• **Goal setting – Record It.** When you have your attitude on straight, it is fitting to keep a journal. Write your story, what you need to accomplish, fears that you need to overcome, progress (milestones) you have made. This is for two reasons. First of all, it is for you to keep the progress of your recently discovered journey. Secondly, write to give yourself a pat on your shoulder for what you have come to accomplish. You may need to share lessons to others how you defeated your fears. Individuals are looking or longing for stories from genuine ordinary individuals like you and me who are heroes, simply like David versus Goliath.

• **Link to Goals.** You might need to take a look at your Personal Spending Planner™ where you list all your family needs, all costs, so this is the place the tyre hits the tar (get genuine with self) where certain luxurious details, must be sacrificed for a while (which is a part that individuals are not ready to do) until you get over this trouble, eg. cut takeaways (dining out), rather bring a lunch pack to work, cut off memberships, for example, DSTV (cable television) rather read books or go to the library (may offer FREE wireless internet) and search for chances to get more cash-flow online (create side hustles). I find that the more dedicated you are, it is amazing the number of imaginative ideas, out of the blue, spring up in your mind. The most important message to get across over is getting Buy-in from your family members (if you are a single parent get your children for assistance; whenever married, approach your mate and youngsters for help). When you have every one of them ready, it lifts the weight off and the reward is that they may even be eager to assist and it makes life so much simpler. You inhale and rest much better around the evening time.

• **Cut up Credit Cards with Scissors** – Instantly, decide that you will quit buying on credit, Period. The initial step is to cut up every one of those extravagant gold cards and this is a demonstration of responsibility to your journey and that you are done and tidied with the elephant in the room. It is additionally a confirmation that you are setting out on a groundbreaking journey to stop using credit obligation to legitimize your focused way of life, that makes a decent try to impress others when in fact you can't pay anything in real cash – that is the thing that is truly going on here. Here it is people, in the event that you can't afford to pay money for it, it is anything but easy to put it on credit card and pay it later. However what you don't understand is that, as long as you keep piling it up, you will wind right back and soak in more into a cycle of debt and you are likewise welcoming "unintended consequences into your own home to live with you until the end of time.

• **Sell Your Stuff.** Throughout the years, we have collected a great deal of stuff around the house that we don't use or they have lost its value, simply check out the house and accumulate clothes, shoes, bags, bits of furniture, iPad, PC, additional vehicles, Televisions sets, camera's, jewelry and offer it to somebody who might be interested to buy, you can have a garage sale or we have such a significant number of internet sites nowadays, that sells "stuff", eBay, Etsy, Facebook (marketplace), Amazon, Cash Converters (locally), utilize this cash to satisfy and pay a portion of your obligation.

• **Sell Your Assets**. With this methodology, I encourage you to take advice from a qualified financial advisor or approach a credit provider before satisfying your credit obligation and don't take cash from your retirement plan (fund) like we see where individuals leave their jobs (occupation) so they can gain access to the pension/provident fund expected to settle some credit obligation (short-lived answer for long term issue), we don't suggest that activity by any means, as it may end up with serious negative disastrous result. The subsequent choice, is taking out a second mortgage (risky) on your home credit, except if, you will be trained enough to stop the cycle of over-spending, else you will be drawn right back in and you would prefer not to put the most significant asset your own roof over yourself and adored ones in risk, so you should ensure it is so worth it, to secure your family. The last alternative is maybe, to take a look at selling your investments (although the interest might be low) check with the financial advisor to ensure you are settling on the correct choice. In addition, there is no reason for saving while you are carrying a substantial debt load with high-loan costs.

• **Start with the Smallest Credit Balance Towards the Biggest.** I call it a stacking strategy and others call it snowballing impact, here is what we need to make snappy successes, force and take advantage of "lower hanging fruits". By attacking the littlest credit obligation first, you need to be so centered around each little obligation in turn and you use every one of those steps mentioned above to pay it off, so once the first is done, you at that point take that installment and you apply it to the following second littlest obligation and stack it as far as possible up until you dispose off the enormous obligation with high interest. Along these same lines, you will be so caught up in the momentum (because you are seeing a significant leap forward) that you will have the option to clear others off faster. Warning, this works on an assumption that you are committed (ALL-IN) regardless of what happens, sure there will be disruptions that go over your way, such as a reality, you need to manage it, however, remain centered around the end goal (reward). As you pay one obligation off, you can give yourself a pat on the back for your achievement, presently you see why it is important to keep the diary, since you can even, write down the dates when the obligations were paid and that you likewise got a paid-up letter from your creditor (they will return to tempt you offering higher points of credit limits and stunningly better-marked cards), remain the course, once that occurs, don't go back, opening up the injury of the difficult painful past and begin the cycle once again, it harms you, yet it sells out the trust of those you cherish and request their help in the first place.

• **Make a Rainy Day Kitty or Emergency Fund.** Do you know Murphy's Law? I don't know who he is and where he comes from, however have you seen that everything that turns out badly will turn out badly, so be set up for some curveballs to be thrown your direction, for example, vehicle breaking down, unplanned costly restorative medical procedure, geyser bursting. We propose that you set aside some cash in a "kitty bag" for rainy days. Keep in mind the sacrifices you made on your financial budget or when you sold some stuff, or some obligation that you may have paid off, it takes into consideration some extra money opportunity that has opened up or a side hustle that is generating some cash, you can use this accessible asset set it aside and continue to make R1 500 ($1 000) to begin with and then increase it over the long run, so it can help when the money gets too tight in the future.

• **Never Neglect to Give and Serve Other People Who Need Help the Most.** On your approach to reaching freedom, it is important that we stop to consider the individuals who are less lucky than us. When we were once paying off our debts, we couldn't give as much as we might want to, so to pay-it-forward (never reap before planting). You need to relate to your hobbies that interest you and give cash or give food parcels or serve or give your time, just to connect with somebody who needs support. By taking part in such exercises, you welcome more noteworthy consistent opportunities, stunning individuals and more blessings into your life and I accept there are conscious co-incidences, nothing occurs by chance (accident).

I might want to leave you with this, make use of the approach that suits your financial pocket or your circumstance, this is in no way, shape or form a one-size-fits-all intentional voluntary debt plan. We additionally understand that this is an extremely sensitive subject and we don't take it lightly. Be as it may, we accept that you at any rate attempt and make a move to change the critical circumstance of your life, it is better to doing nothing by any means, as this would lead you to a far more disastrous condition. Towards the finish, all things considered, it is your decision, do what works for you.

ABOUT THE AUTHOR

Zinzi Mdedetyana born and bred in the Southern Tip of Africa (South Africa) is an emerging author. She is a financial wellness mentor and a member of COMENSA (Coaches & Mentors of South Africa). She is a board member of COMETSA Heritage Development Agency NPC serving on the Finance Committee.

As Managing Director of Zealous Royalty Ark Pty Limited (home for managing personal finances), she finds ways to help and guide her clients to reduce their financial stress so they may experience personal financial balance, abundance, and well-being. She does so by engaging and identifying a client's financial profile (journey) through nourishing authentic yet respectful conversations that address their fears.

Get in touch with Zinzi at www.royaltyark.com.

f facebook.com/zinzi.mdedetyana

www.ingramcontent.com/pod-product-compliance
Lightning Source LLC
Chambersburg PA
CBHW070935210326
41520CB00021B/6952